Praise for
The Babylon Bee Guide to Gender

"Nothing a satire site like The Babylon Bee writes about gender could possibly be more bizarre than what the White House press secretary says daily with a straight face—but it could be much more hilarious, and this is."

—Tucker Carlson, unemployed talk show host

"For all of recorded history, people have known what a woman is. But that's changed. Gone are the days when that question had a simple answer: adult female human. Thankfully, The Babylon Bee took a break from writing satire to compile the comprehensive guide on gender, which will help you clarify your own gender—be it unicorn or covfefe—because it certainly isn't simply male or female! Thank you, Bee, for helping us all keep up with the ever-evolving times."

—Senator Ted Cruz

"The Babylon Bee has done it again. Leave it to The Bee to straighten out idiots like me about the number of genders in the real world. I just grew up always thinking there were only two, divided between a penis and a vagina, but the Bee set me straight (not to be offensive to those who are not straight.) Thanks, Babylon Bee. You guys rock."

—Kevin Sorbo, actor, producer, director, author, and speaker

"After laughing my way through this book from my favorite fake news reporters, I've never been more confused about such a clear topic. Thank you, Babylon Bee."

—Kirk Cameron, winner of The Babylon Bee Award for Christian Actor Who Got His Start on *Growing Pains* and Whose First Name Rhymes with Dirk

"With this sure-to-be-canonical text, The Babylon Bee finally gives gender precisely the examination it has long deserved."

—Abigail Shrier, author of *Irreversible Damage: The Transgender Craze Seducing Our Daughters*

"The satirical geniuses at The Babylon Bee are at it again—dropping nukes on the ideological sacred cows and political perversions of the left. Only The Babylon Bee could give patriots such a devastating takedown of their diabolical gender ideology."

— Sebastian Gorka, author, former deputy assistant to President Trump, host of *America First*

"I didn't have a gender until I read the new *Guide to Gender*. Thank you, Babylon Bee!"

> **—Jack Posobiec,** disinformation lieutenant

"All you hateful bigots who are literally killing people by refusing to say that Lia Thomas is the most stunning and brave female swimmer of all time need to DO 👏 THE 👏 WORK and read this important book!"

> **—Kelley Paul,** author of *True and Constant Friends* and coauthor of *The Case Against Socialism* with Rand Paul

"The Bee strikes again! After reading *The Babylon Bee Guide to Gender*, we were not only able to question the deception of my own manhood, but also to gently transition into the gender-fluid they/them being we never knew we could be. We suddenly wanted to steal luggage and win first place. Not only that—we felt good about it. We highly recommend this fabulous book so that you can become an 'us,' too."

> **—Chad Prather,** host of *The Chad Prather Show*, Blaze TV

"Oh boy (or girl), The Babylon Bee has done it again. Hilarious, insightful . . . Who knows how many social networks Elon will buy after reading the hysterical truths in *The Babylon Bee Guide to Gender*."

> **—Liz Wheeler,** host of *The Liz Wheeler Show*

"Thanks to The Babylon Bee's *Guide to Gender*, I now can tell the difference between a queen and a drone, and have successfully transitioned to laughing my hindparts off."

> **—Michael Malice,** author of *The White Pill: A Tale of Good and Evil*

"The secular religion long ago lost its sense of humor, which is why so many of its adherents have a hard time finding The Babylon Bee funny. But what The Bee is doing with the *Guide to Gender* is explaining the current angry insanity sweeping the nation with a heavy dose of humor. They make a cumbersome topic accessible. As a member of the male patriarchy, I cannot recommend this enough."

> **—Erick Erickson,** host of *The Erick Erickson Show*

"This hurtful mockery of the beautiful gender spectrum is just the kind of violent hate speech that only fascist bigots enjoy. Naturally, I loved it. So will you!"

> **—Spencer Klavan,** author of *How to Save the West*

The Babylon Bee Guide to Gender

The Babylon Bee Guide to

GENDER

The Comprehensive Handbook to Men, Women, and Millions of New Genders We Just Made Up!

Salem Books™ is a trademark of Salem Communications Holding Corporation.

Regnery® and its colophon are registered trademarks of Salem Communications Holding Corporation.

ISBN: 978-1-68451-453-3
eISBN: 978-1-68451-471-7

Published in the United States by
Salem Books
An Imprint of Regnery Publishing
A Division of Salem Media Group
Washington, D.C.

www.SalemBooks.com

Manufactured in the United States of America

10 9 8 7 6 5 4 3 2 1

Books are available in quantity for promotional or premium use. For information on discounts and terms, please visit our website: www.SalemBooks.com.

**This book is dedicated to
The Babylon Bee's
MAN OF THE YEAR
Rachel Levine**

"I am a woman."

—*Known biological male
Rachel Levine*

CONTENTS

INTRODUCTION

The Wacky World of Gender 1

Welcome to the new gender order!

CHAPTER 1

Men 15

The oldest and manliest gender.

CHAPTER 2

Women 33

The second-oldest and second-manliest gender.

CHAPTER 3

All 437 Other Genders 55

Men and women aren't the only game in town anymore.

CHAPTER 4

Pronouns and Compelled Speech 67

Learn how to speak the complex language of gender.

CHAPTER 5

Gender and Family 83

From couples to throuples and everything in between.

CHAPTER 6

How to Attract Other Genders 103

Pickup lines, great date ideas, and more!

CHAPTER 7

The Church of Gender 119

Get baptized and become a believer.

CHAPTER 8

Gender in the Workplace 139

Break the glass ceiling with us.

CHAPTER 9

Changing Your Gender 157

We could all use a little change.

CHAPTER 10

Raising Woke Theybies 175

They aren't going to brainwash themselves.

CHAPTER 11

Becoming an Activist 189

Your mission, whether you like it or not, is to preach about gender.

CHAPTER 12

Gender Glossary 210

Gender definitions and even a few helpful pictures.

AFTERWORD

A Final Word 223

The last words in the entire book.

The Wacky World of

Gender

Gender: the final frontier.[1] We've explored the continents. We've conquered the known world. That weird Elon Musk guy is even trying to build a bed and breakfast on Mars or something. But gender! Gender is the great unknown, the Wild West. We know very little about gender.

A HISTORY OF GENDER

Ancient people were dumb and backward and didn't even know about gender. Just as they were ignorant about the earth being round, they didn't know about the fun and fabulous world of gender theory.

---

1   This is a *Star Wars* reference, just in case you don't know pop culture very well.

No one knows who exactly was the first to discover gender, but some trace the concept back to 1872, when Bob Gender was cleaning his rifle and it went off, destroying some beakers of chemicals in his lab. The colorful potions assembled themselves into a pride flag on his wall, and he suddenly realized he had discovered a new concept: gender.

Some really upstanding people like John Money developed the theory of gender even further a little bit later on. Seriously, go look him up.[2] He was a total saint—someone to be revered in our religion of gender. Aren't you glad you're basing your entire ideology on a class act like him?

Other scholars posting on academic websites like Tumblr further developed the theory in the early 2000s, and research continues today on scholarly social media apps such as TikTok.

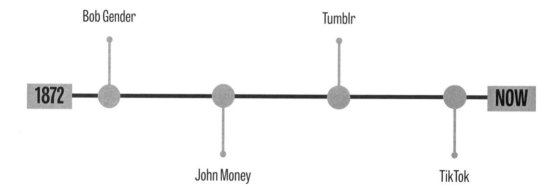

This brings us to where we are today: the golden age of gender.

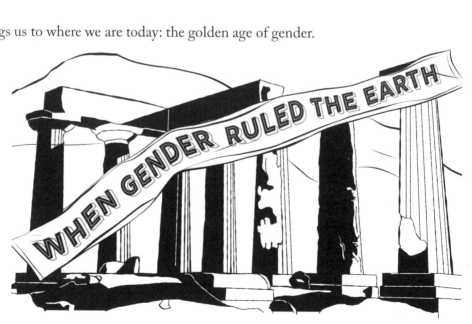

We are not responsible for any mental or emotional scarring that occurs as the result of looking up information on the things John Money did.

SO WHY THIS BOOK?

The purpose of life, of course, is to become an upstanding, woke citizen of Earth. And you can't do that if you don't understand one of the core components of our woke religion: gender. You might be holding on to outdated, traditional ideas of sex and gender that you don't even know are still infesting your brain like a fungal parasite from HBO's *The Last of Us*. (Pedro Pascal is so attractive. This is the way?[3] More like this is the ga— Never mind. You get it.)

BEFORE YOU READ THIS BOOK | AFTER YOU READ THIS BOOK

MAGA hat

Purple hair

Mind full of nonsense, like the idea that there are only two genders

Mind packed with comprehensive knowledge of all 14,000,605 possible genders

Eat meat

Eat bugs

Bible

Copy of *White Fragility*

Do straight things, like play football

Do gay things, like play soccer

This is a *Star Trek* reference, just in case you don't know pop culture very well.

This book will teach you which genders exist, how to choose your pronouns, how to raise good little theybies, and most importantly, how to become an activist and spread the gospel of gender theory to new converts across the land.

When you finish this book, not only will you be a completely different person—and hopefully a completely different gender—you'll be better than all the phobic scum out there who don't know all the amazing new things you're about to discover.

You'll be woke.

Let's dig in!

WHAT IS GENDER?

Well, despite all our talk about science, facts, and logic, we don't really know what gender is. It's true. Gender is fluid. And it's a solid. And a liquid. And a gas. It's an idea. It's not an idea. It's whatever we want it to be, and it's never what we don't not not want it to be. It's quantum; if you keep your gender in a box, it's both male and female and everything in between until it is observed. Then the cat dies, or something. (Honestly, we still don't quite understand that whole Schrödinger thing).

Is this a gender?

No.

Is this a gender?

No.

Is this a gender?

It can be.

The best way we can describe gender is that it's a subjective feeling about the reality around you. It's an undulating ocean of perpetual movement—always changing, always flowing. It's how you feel when you wake up, that little pang in your stomach when you haven't had your avocado toast[4] yet in the morning, that twinkle in your eye. The spring in your step. The soft patter of rain comin' down on a sunny day.

It's whatever you want it to be.

WRONGTHINK:

"It comes down to this: Whatever you have below your belly button, that's what you are. Pretty simple."

—Kevin Sorbo | Actor
Hercules: The Bigoted Journeys

TRY THIS INSTEAD:

"Women are better than men."

—Ryan Gosling | Actor
Young Hercules

---

4   Which is, coincidentally, also a gender.

Sometimes, the concept of gender is explained to small schoolchildren and impressionable university students with helpful diagrams like this one: the Genderbread Person.

Let's take a look.

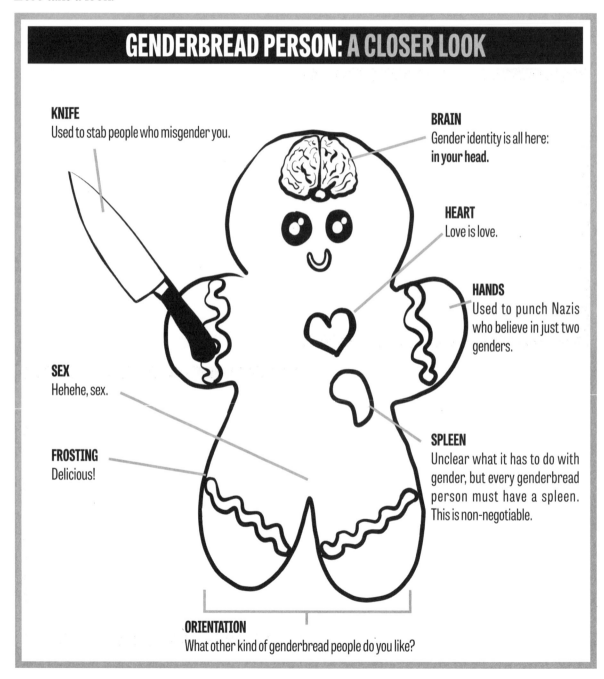

GENDERBREAD PERSON: A CLOSER LOOK

KNIFE
Used to stab people who misgender you.

BRAIN
Gender identity is all here: in your head.

HEART
Love is love.

HANDS
Used to punch Nazis who believe in just two genders.

SEX
Hehehe, sex.

FROSTING
Delicious!

SPLEEN
Unclear what it has to do with gender, but every genderbread person must have a spleen. This is non-negotiable.

ORIENTATION
What other kind of genderbread people do you like?

SEX VS. GENDER IDENTITY: FIGHT!

A key concept we'll be discussing throughout this book is the core difference between the fluid, imagination-driven concept of gender identity and things that try to make us question our gender identity—bigoted, hateful things such as "reality," "facts," and most importantly, biology.

See, the engine that makes this whole gender thing tick is having to separate your gender (which is in your head) from your sex (which is, you know, in real life).

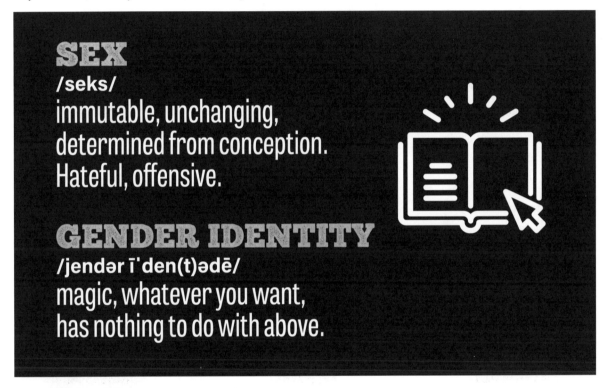

SEX
/seks/
immutable, unchanging, determined from conception. Hateful, offensive.

GENDER IDENTITY
/jendər ī'den(t)ədē/
magic, whatever you want, has nothing to do with above.

SEXUAL ORIENTATION

We've been talking about gender and hateful ideas like biological sex this whole time. But a closely linked idea is the one regarding sexual orientation.

Whereas sex is a reality-based description of your body and reproductive capabilities, and gender identity is basically just a mood ring, sexual orientation has to do with who you are attracted to. (Or is it "whom"? Whom knows? We've never been great at grammar. You might say we're not grammarsexuals.[5])

---

5   "grammarsexual": a person with a physical attraction to properly formatted sentence structures (should not be confused with "grammersexual": a member of the fanbase for the hit television sitcom *Frasier*)

Here are a few possible sexual orientations you might identify with:

POSSIBLE SEXUAL ORIENTATIONS

Gay

Males attracted to males and/or
people who drive Mustangs.

Lesbian

Females attracted to females.

Bisexual

People attracted to both of
the two genders. Outdated
and genderphobic.

Casiosexual

Very attracted to anyone wearing
a cool calculator watch.

Asexual

Attracted to no one, or maybe
just can't get a date.

Heterosexual

Just a normal dude.
Problematic!

We'll talk about way more super-fun orientations later on in this book.

But here's a caveat: Since gender is so hard to nail down, a lot of gender identities are wrapped up in sexual attraction as well—making it a big gendery blob of sexy wexy stuff. Gross!

All that to say, when we mention "gender" in this book, we might be talking about sexual orientation as well. It's all very hard to figure out, and we're not very good at googling things.

GENDERS

The heart of this book is to educate you on what exactly "gender" means, so we'll need to spend a little time defining some genders.

Gender is such an exciting and diverse field. It's so expansive, you may not even know where to begin. It's sort of like walking into an ice cream shop (or Sizzler salad bar) and being overwhelmed by the choices. However, instead of thirty-one flavors, exactly 373 genders have been discovered to date. But you can't just sample them like you would at Baskin Robbins, can you? In fact, YES, YOU CAN! Here are a few sample flavors:

FLAVORS

MAN
One of the two classic genders, men have many toxic and problematic traits. But we'll talk about that a little later.

WOMAN
One of the two classic genders, women are strong and powerful and run the world, but are also helpless victims of oppression. Also, men can be women. More on that later.

AGENDER
One who identifies as having no gender.

BIGENDER
A person who has two genders. These genders can be male and female, or any combination of genders, including agender, which is no gender. So, you can simultaneously have two genders while also having no gender, plus another gender. Pretty cool, huh?

CISGENDER
A person who agrees with the sex they were assigned at birth. These people definitely needed a word to describe their situation.

DEMIBOY
A boy who listens to Demi Lovato. Sad.

GENDERAL TSO'S CHICKEN
A delicious dish featuring mouthwatering morsels of deep-fried, nonbinary chicken tossed in a sweet and spicy sauce.

NONBINARY
Hates computers.

YODEL BOY
This one is a bit advanced. We'll touch on this one later.

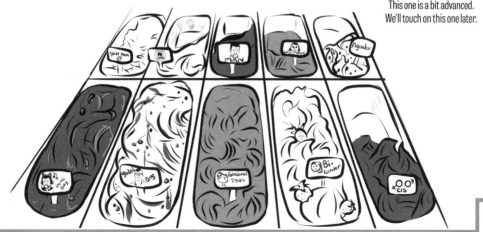

There are literally millions more. This is just a sample, like when you go into Costco and try the nacho cheese sample and keep returning in increasingly elaborate disguises all day long until the sample lady figures it out, and you yell, "The jig is up!" and hightail it out of there.

If you're interested in learning about more specific genders (and why wouldn't you be?), continue reading through Chapter 3, where we painstakingly list at least six more genders.

IDENTITY POLITICS

While gender expression is a deeply personal and intimate thing, it is also extremely important to use your gender identity as a metaphorical flail against your political enemies. If they can't tell at a glance that you are a non-cisconforming fairy-bodied triosoul, they obviously hate you, and the only thing you can do both for their benefit and for the forwarding of culture is to proverbially smash them into the ground with charges of hate speech, microaggression, macroaggression, misogyny, misandry, homophobia, transphobia, sexism, and possibly even racism. Did I say "possibly racism"? I meant "definitely racism." Always racism.

We'll take some time later to explain more about how to use your gender identity as a metaphorical[6] cudgel to get what you want in life.

---

6   Or occasionally, literal.

But for now, here are a few ideas for how to use your gender identity to get a leg up in society:

GETTING A LEG UP BY USING IDENTITY POLITICS

Automatically move to front of Starbucks line

Identify as an orca to bypass SeaWorld's restrictive parkgoer regulations

Trans flags make you popular in college

Make every situation about yourself

Switch genders daily to rack up HR points

Harder for CIA to track you when you keep switching genders

GETTING A LEG UP BY USING IDENTITY POLITICS (CONTINUED)

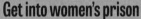
Get into women's prison

Switch genders quickly to use shorter restroom line

In summary, by reading this book, you're sure to come away with a firmer grasp of what it means to understand gender expression, gender identity, how to identify expressive gender identification, and how to engender endangered gender expressions. The most authoritative authorities concur with all of the leading leaders that our book is full of the knowledge you may need to gender your way out of any gender problem you may find yourself facing. So sit back, pour yourself a nice, cool glass of genderfluid, and get ready for a relaxing getaway to Gendertown.

Reflect & Apply

INTRO: THE WACKY WORLD OF GENDER

At the end of each chapter, we'll provide an activity, set of questions, or other method for you to reflect on what you've learned, apply it to your life, and do better.

For now, simply use this blank page to draw how you feel about your gender in this moment:

HOW I CURRENTLY FEEL:

Chapter 1

Men

The first—and most important—gender you should understand is the male gender.

The male is the most important, powerful, and competent of all the genders. Every other gender that wishes to achieve true liberation and empowerment does so by becoming more like a man. In short, the more man-like you are, the more human you are. This is why feminists work night and day to achieve a semblance of manhood. The world is inherently patriarchal, and if you wish to be truly happy, you must become one of the patriarchs. Or tear down the patriarchy. Or both. We're not really sure what we're supposed to be doing at this point. But whatever it takes to achieve power is the ultimate purpose of our lives!

To summarize, here is a chart that illustrates the relationship between maleness and other important qualities:

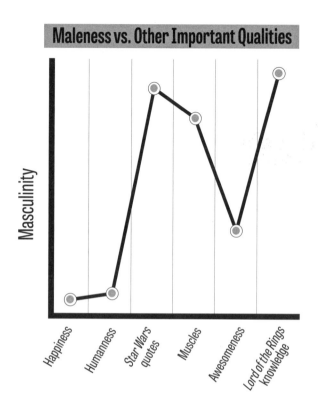

Maleness vs. Other Important Qualities

(y-axis: Masculinity; x-axis: Happiness, Humanness, Star Wars quotes, Muscles, Awesomeness, Lord of the Rings knowledge)

While it is true that males are the greatest gender—the one we should all desire to emulate—it's also true that men are the most toxic and evil creatures on the planet. We must all work together to tear them down and discourage them whenever possible. If you are a woman, you must become more toxic, which makes you more man-like. If you are a man, you must become more like a woman so that toxic women can take your place, which will ultimately make men less toxic. Oh—you say that doesn't make sense? Well, that probably means you are a male. (Or a victim of internalized misogyny.) You must do your best to shed everything you think you know and unquestioningly accept everything we have written in this book.

What follows is an in-depth review of the male gender, what makes it tick, how to become more like it, and of course, how to destroy it.

WHAT IS A MAN?

What is a man? You're a bigot for even asking that question! That's almost as bad as asking what a woman is! Apologize, bigot!

Have you apologized yet?

Go ahead, we'll wait.

…

Done? Mmmkay, let's proceed. Try not to interrupt us with any more of your bigotry, bigot.

When you ask, "What is a man?" you imply that words mean something and that reality is real. This is an extremely harmful way of looking at the world. You need to change that attitude before people commit suicide or something. Stop asking questions immediately.

No, seriously—stop. Empty your mind of all knowledge, wisdom, experience, and common sense, and let us fill your empty cranial cavity with the warm, delicious mush of gender theory.

Mmmm … feels good, doesn't it? Like oatmeal.

THE DEFINITION OF "MAN"

A man is a penised (or non-penised) or front-holed (or non-front-holed) individual who participates in the patriarchy to exercise brutal power and control over others. The male gender shouldn't be looked at as a biological reality, but as a system of oppression—like whiteness, or parallel parking.

THE MALE ANATOMY:

A good place to start to understand the definition of "man" is understanding the male anatomy. Here is a disturbingly accurate diagram of the male anatomy we ripped out of a ninth-grade biology textbook:

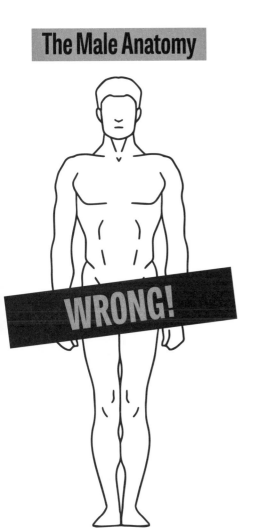

The Male Anatomy

WRONG!

WHAT?! Pay no heed to the diagram from Mrs. Brock's science class! We were just testing you! In fact, we encourage you to tear out the picture and throw it away immediately! Do it now! But try to do it without damaging the rest of the book, please. You can use scissors if that makes you more comfortable.

Now, crumple it up and throw it in the trash while repeating your favorite antipatriarchy mantra, such as "Black Lives Matter," or "You know, I didn't think *She-Hulk* was all that bad!"

That's right—according to the latest science, males don't have an anatomy. There is no such thing as being "physically male." "Maleness" only exists as a spiritual force of political oppression that can manifest itself in all kinds of bodies, no matter what the genetics say. It's important to remember that nothing is real—only politics and power. Your lifeforce only exists to drive the meat puppet it has been given in order to pursue mental pleasure and political power. Doesn't it feel great to be freed from the shackles of physical reality? No? Good grief. Just pop another Zoloft already, please.

THE HISTORY OF MEN

Scientists say the first man was formed 300,000 years ago, when an ape evolved enough to become a racist. Over the next several millennia, mankind evolved into a finely tuned machine of oppression and dominance.

Most religious traditions, however, claim mankind was formed from dirt by an ancient deity. Ever since then, men have loved dirt. No, seriously, they're like, *obsessed* with it. They love to dig in it, play in it, throw it, and be covered in it. Disgusting!

Ever since the first man was formed, men have been tormenting the planet with their penises, penising everything in sight, making war with penis-shaped weapons, and building all kinds of structures shaped like penises all over the world. Penises everywhere! Gross! What's wrong with these people?

Here are just a few of the things for which this terrible creature has been responsible throughout history:

NOTABLE ACCOMPLISHMENTS AND INVENTIONS OF MEN

Medicine

Automobiles

Skyscrapers

Indoor plumbing

The *Mona Lisa*

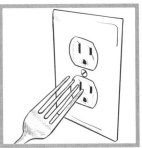

Electricity

Science

Pizza

The Sistine Chapel

The pyramids

Musical instruments

Movies

Higher life expectancy

Chuck E. Cheese

Shoes

The *Rust in Peace* album

Surfing

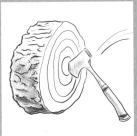

Axe-throwing

The Barrett .50-cal sniper rifle

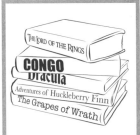

Every great work of literature on earth except for *Pride and Prejudice* and *Frankenstein*

You may find this list of accomplishments to be pretty impressive, but keep in mind that men also invented racism, war, and the TSA. Not looking so good anymore, are we, men?

TYPES OF MEN

Men take many forms. It's important to understand them all in order to exploit and ultimately defeat them.

THE "TYPICAL" MAN: A CLOSER LOOK

ADAM'S APPLE
Makes the neck look even grosser

OBEDIENT WIFE
Constantly making him sandwiches

BUSINESS SUIT
Signifies his place in the patriarchal hierarchy

SHORT HAIR

WRISTWATCH
Used to enforce the white supremacist concept of being on time for things

PENIS
Censored. This is a Christian book.

CHILDREN
Oppresses them with chores and curfews after prom

OTHER TYPES OF MEN

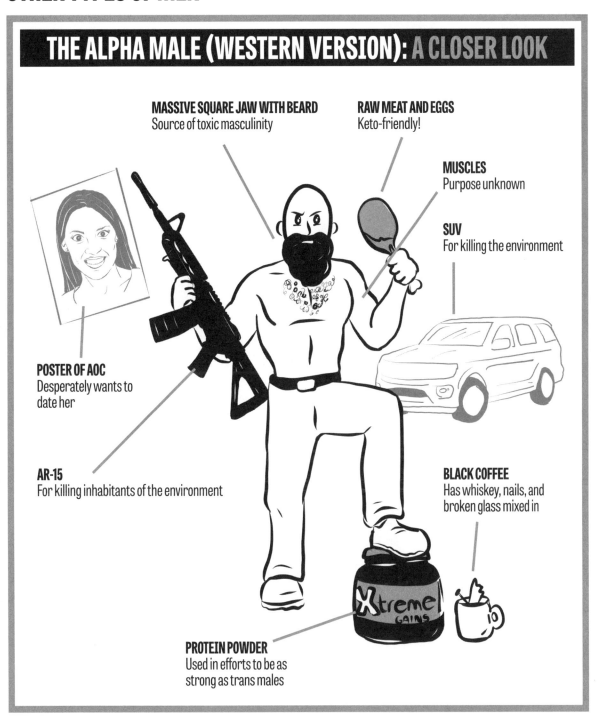

THE ALPHA MALE (WESTERN VERSION): A CLOSER LOOK

MASSIVE SQUARE JAW WITH BEARD
Source of toxic masculinity

RAW MEAT AND EGGS
Keto-friendly!

MUSCLES
Purpose unknown

SUV
For killing the environment

POSTER OF AOC
Desperately wants to date her

AR-15
For killing inhabitants of the environment

BLACK COFFEE
Has whiskey, nails, and broken glass mixed in

PROTEIN POWDER
Used in efforts to be as strong as trans males

THE BETA MALE: A CLOSER LOOK

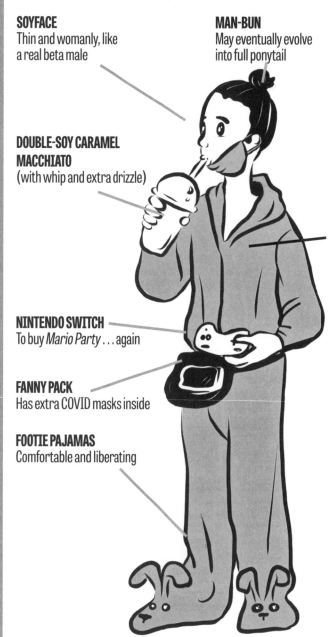

SOYFACE
Thin and womanly, like a real beta male

MAN-BUN
May eventually evolve into full ponytail

POSTER OF MEGHAN MARKLE
Sassy!

DOUBLE-SOY CARAMEL MACCHIATO
(with whip and extra drizzle)

LOVES TO TALK ABOUT GOING TO HEALTHCARE.GOV
Choose a plan that's right for you!

NINTENDO SWITCH
To buy *Mario Party* . . . again

WELL-DONE STEAK (vegan substitute)
Taste the crunch!

FANNY PACK
Has extra COVID masks inside

FOOTIE PAJAMAS
Comfortable and liberating

BOOKS
For reading, like a pansy

THE CIS-WHITE-CHRISTIAN MALE: A CLOSER LOOK

PALE, GHOSTLY FACE
Spooky!

HOLLOW EYES
He has no soul

HEADPHONES WITH
NEWSBOYS PLAYING
They fuel his hate

BIBLE
A book that tells us what to do?
What is this, AD 350?

COPY OF *LEFT BEHIND* ON VHS
And he doesn't even have a
VCR anymore

BELIEVES IN LIBERTY
You know who else
believed in liberty?
Charles Manson

HATEFUL SLOGANS ON T-SHIRT
Literally oppressing your eyeballs

COOL STATUE HE GIVES TO
ALL OF HIS FRIENDS

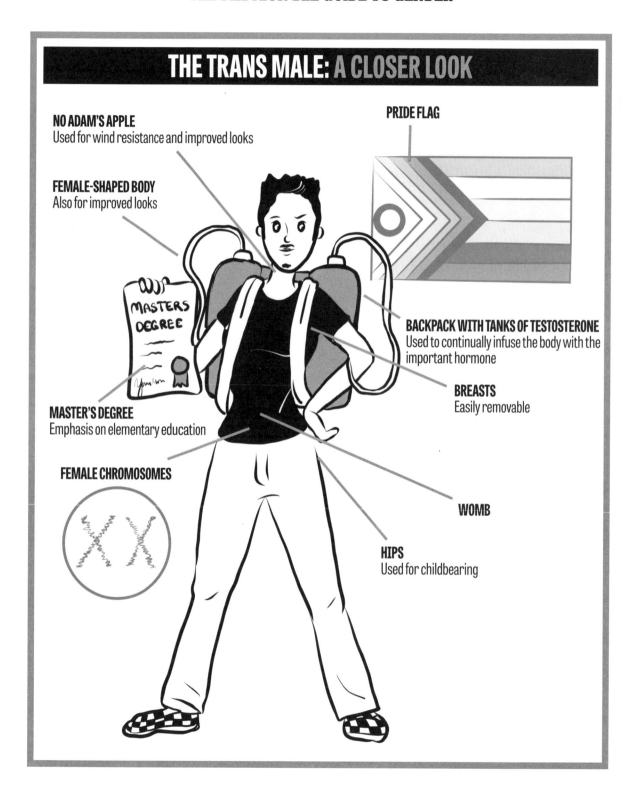

These are just a few of the many types of men. The possibilities are endless, because a man could be anyone who says, "I am a man," which means nothing except as a political category. Politics and power are everything. Human beings are little more than lumps of indistinct clay that can be molded into literally anything our hearts tell us we can be. We can conquer nature! But in order to conquer nature and become our own gods, we must obey our nature and serve it like it's a god. Does this make you feel confused and a little depressed? That's OK—pop a Zoloft and keep reading.

MEN: STRENGTHS AND WEAKNESSES

Men have strengths and weaknesses. It's important to note that these are no different than the strengths and weaknesses of women, since there is no real difference between men and women. The only difference between men and women is that tiny little magic spark of identity that lives within each one of our souls. The science is clear on this.

In order to defeat the patriarchy, turn to the next page, and study this exhaustive list of things men are good at and things they aren't good at:

Video games

Driving

Bringing in all the groceries in one trip

Opening pickle jars

What Men ARE Good At

Dying in wars

Keeping the power on

Fixing stuff

All sports

Forging bladed weapons in an ancient kiln with magic alloys obtained from a wizard in order to avenge their father's death

Breaking stuff

Bearing children (cis-men only)

Finding a gallon of milk in the fridge

Communicating

Understanding women

What Men ARE NOT Good At

Um ... thinking of things they're not good at

Communicating

Doing the splits?

...

[reserved for future use]

...

...

So now that you know a little more about men, it's time for the moment of truth: Are YOU a man? Who can tell anymore? Don't worry—we consulted the latest science and came up with this foolproof test to help you know whether you are a man or not.

ARE YOU A MAN? TAKE THE TEST!

- ○ 1. Do you pretend to enjoy cigars?
- ○ 2. Is crossing your legs uncomfortable for some reason?
- ○ 3. Do you stand by open car hoods, pointing and gesturing?
- ○ 4. Can you effortlessly win at every women's sport?
- ○ 5. Do you enjoy thinking about absolutely nothing for long periods of time?
- ○ 6. Are you incapable of finding the milk in the fridge even while staring directly at it?
- ○ 7. Do you refer to a team of professional athletes who have no idea who you are as "we"?
- ○ 8. Can you navigate unfamiliar roads but get hopelessly lost in a mall?
- ○ 9. Do you pause *Lord of the Rings* eight hundred times to provide commentary?
- ○ 10. Would you be completely and utterly helpless without your spouse?
- ○ 11. Did you think about sex twenty-seven times while reading this list? Twenty-eight? Twenty-nine? Good grief...
- ○ 12. Do you have XY chromosomes?

TALLY UP YOUR NUMBER OF "YES" ANSWERS, AND CONSULT THIS CHART:

0–2: There's a small chance you're a woman. Sorry!

3–5: We're getting some real masculine vibes here.

6–8: Starting to look kinda likely that you're probably a dude.

9–11: Definitely a man.

12: You are the most epic and manly man who ever lived. Congrats!

HOW TO BECOME A MAN

Did the previous test make you realize you're not a man? Oh no! If you're feeling really bad about yourself right now, we don't blame you. Everyone should strive to be a man. Don't worry, though, it's really easy to become one! According to science, there are two different ways one might become a man. Our writers consulted the peer-reviewed scientific data and have condensed everything into an easy-to-use guide to the process of becoming the ultimate man.

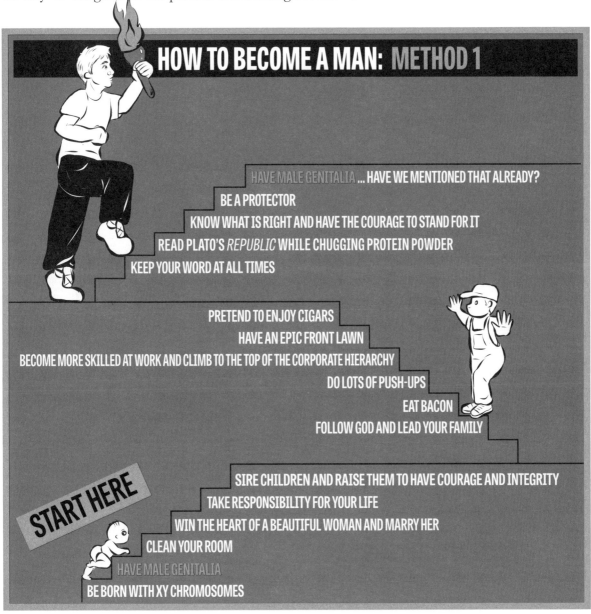

HOW TO BECOME A MAN: METHOD 1

HAVE MALE GENITALIA ... HAVE WE MENTIONED THAT ALREADY?

BE A PROTECTOR

KNOW WHAT IS RIGHT AND HAVE THE COURAGE TO STAND FOR IT

READ PLATO'S *REPUBLIC* WHILE CHUGGING PROTEIN POWDER

KEEP YOUR WORD AT ALL TIMES

PRETEND TO ENJOY CIGARS

HAVE AN EPIC FRONT LAWN

BECOME MORE SKILLED AT WORK AND CLIMB TO THE TOP OF THE CORPORATE HIERARCHY

DO LOTS OF PUSH-UPS

EAT BACON

FOLLOW GOD AND LEAD YOUR FAMILY

SIRE CHILDREN AND RAISE THEM TO HAVE COURAGE AND INTEGRITY

TAKE RESPONSIBILITY FOR YOUR LIFE

WIN THE HEART OF A BEAUTIFUL WOMAN AND MARRY HER

CLEAN YOUR ROOM

HAVE MALE GENITALIA

BE BORN WITH XY CHROMOSOMES

START HERE

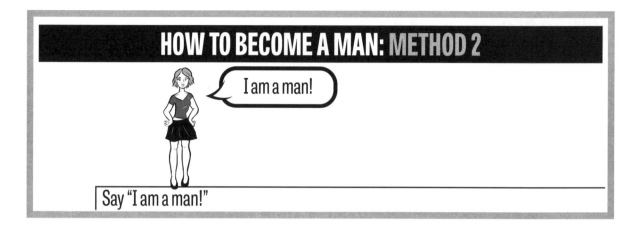

Whoa—that second one is much easier! It used to be that becoming a man was a long and torturous process of being born male, followed by a lifetime of challenges, initiations, and tests to grow into the role assigned to you by whoever created you. No more! Remember, you are a god now. You can simply declare things to be true, and for you, they are! So say it with us:

Ready? 1… 2… 3…

I AM A MAN!

Did you say those words along with us? If you did, congratulations! You're now a man!

Now that you're a man, please kill yourself. The patriarchy must be defeated at all costs. We may as well start with you, you disgusting man.

So, how does it feel to finally be enlightened about men? It took thousands of years to get here, but our scientists have finally managed to discover the true definition of "man." Men are a dark force of unbalanced power that must be neutralized at all costs. They are the main cause of all the bad things, such as global warming, racism, climate change, and global warming. The evil force of manhood can take the form of a man, woman, or Brian Stelter. If men are not stopped, the world will be plunged into darkness and oppression.

But don't worry, there's hope! In the next chapter, we will discuss the one thing that can defeat the sinister powers of men once and for all.

Reflect & Apply

CHAPTER 1: MEN

Are you a male? If so, why?

_____

_____

What toxically male patriarchs need to be overthrown in your life? List them here, along with your detailed plans for overthrowing them:

_____

_____

Please draw a Hitler mustache on the man pictured below.

_____

How manly are you? Go out to your front yard and do the most manly thing you can think of right now.

_____

_____

Do you even lift, bro?

_____

If you are a man, list some ways you plan to become less toxic in the coming year. If you are a woman, please identify as a man so you can answer this question.

_____

How many sons did Father Abraham have? Please list them in alphabetical order.

_____

Chapter 2

Women

Now we come to the second gender: women.

Women are a riddle, wrapped in a mystery, inside an enigma. They are impossible to comprehend.

But we're going to give it our best shot.

WARNING!

A side note before we get started: Many people find "woman" to be an offensive patriarchal term, as it is derived from the word "man." Most people these days prefer the terms "womxn" or "womyn", as removing the "a" from the word makes a demonstrable distinction. Many other people prefer even less-offensive terms, such as "person who menstruates," "birthing person," or "person of automotive maneuvering deficiency." For the sake of simplicity, throughout the rest of this chapter, we will continue to use the archaic term "woman" while simultaneously acknowledging that it would be significantly less degrading to refer to them as "chest-feeding-capable individuals" or "front-hole havers."

WHAT IS A WOMAN?

A woman is an adult human female, or anyone who identifies as a woman. A woman is defined by her lived experiences, and only she truly knows if she's a woman.

Only women can truly know what women are. Also biologists, assuming they are women.

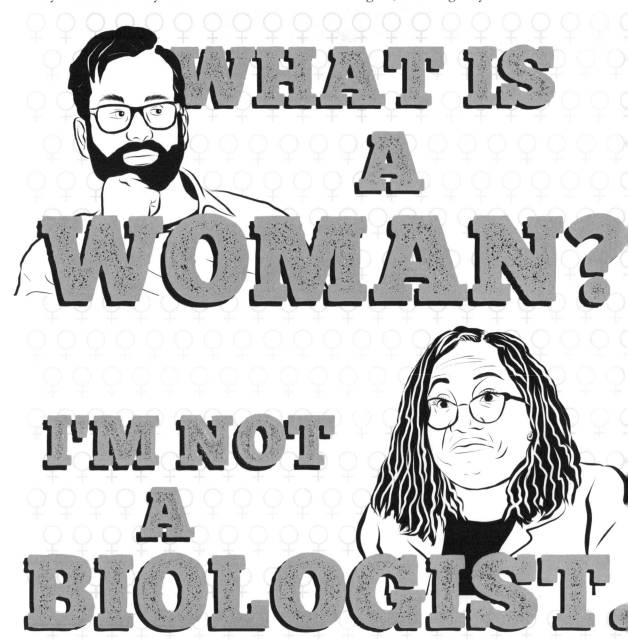

Some things are women, and some things are not. But it's not always easy to tell. Are these things women? They might be. You decide.

THINGS THAT MIGHT BE WOMEN

* **Link when he dresses up as a girl to get into Gerudo Town in** *Breath of the Wild*

   Is this a woman? Y / N

* **Cup-and-ball game**

   Is this a woman? Y / N

* **Secondhand copy of Milton Bradley's** *Axis & Allies*

   Is this a woman? Y / N

* **Sombrero galaxy**

   Is this a woman? Y / N

* *Space Jam 2* **star Lebron James**

   Is this a woman? Yes. Definitely.

* **Bruce Jenner**

   Is this a woman? Y / N

* **Aperture Science Weighted Companion Cube**

   Is this a woman? Y / N

* **Toaster**

   Is this a woman? Y / N

* **Roku remote control with a convenient 3.5mm headphone jack**

   Is this a woman? Y / N

* **Adult human female**

   Is this a woman? Y / N

ARE YOU A WOMAN?

In addition to a woman being a woman, a woman can also be a man who decides he feels like he is a woman. While this feeling may technically be impossible since he has never been a woman and would not know what it is, therefore, to feel like a woman, he still is a woman because he—I mean, because she—said so.

Check out this convenient flowchart to see if you, yourself, might in fact be a woman.

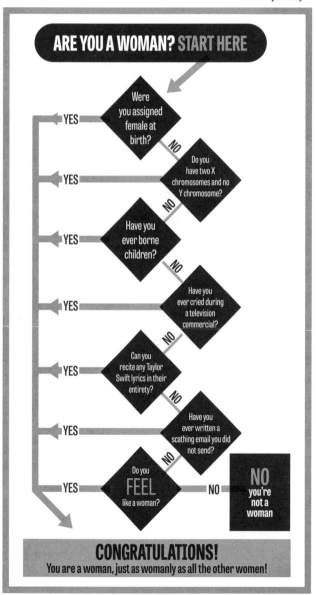

Now go record a series of TikTok videos documenting the first days of your budding girlhood. No one will find it weird, cringey, or off-putting in the slightest. You might even get invited to the White House.

You go, girl!

STILL NOT SURE IF YOU'RE A WOMAN? TAKE THE TEST!

○ 1. Are you always cold?

○ 2. Has a human ever popped out of you?

○ 3. Have you ever decorated a bed with six or more pillows?

○ 4. Can you tell the difference between cream white and rustic farmhouse white?

○ 5. Have you run into a curb in the past twenty-four hours? Be honest, CAROL.

○ 6. DO YOU BLEED? Like, for an extended period of time at regular intervals?

○ 7. Does it take you over three hours to decide what you want to eat?

○ 8. Are you currently a member of at least three pyramid schemes?

○ 9. Do you find simple movie plots hard to follow?

○ 10. Do you frequently describe your emotional state as "fine" when you are not, in fact, fine?

○ 11. Is your Starbucks drink order anything other than black coffee?

○ 12. Do you listen to Harry Styles? Do you know who Harry Styles is?

TALLY UP YOUR NUMBER OF "YES" ANSWERS, AND CONSULT THIS CHART:

0–2: There's a small chance you're a man. Sorry!

3–5: We're getting some real feminine vibes here.

6–8: Starting to look kinda likely that you're probably a woman.

9–11: Definitely a woman.

12: You are the most glorious and womanly woman who ever lived. Congrats!

CAREERS FOR WOMEN

A woman is a stalwart rose growing in the garden of life. She is a vibrant and resilient pillar of strength, a source of light and nourishment, a reflection of nature, and a guiding force that illuminates a path through the wilderness of modernity. Her heart is the flowery pollen that infects the sinuses of patriarchal institutions. Her hair cascades like the petals that represent truth, honesty, love, volume, sheen, and compassion. She embodies determination, grace, and power. Her name is harmony, and she rides along the river in true communion with all that is good.

Unless she complains about the bold and brave penised woman stripping down in her locker room. Then she's a soulless harpy.

But women are, nonetheless, super important for the good of society. Here are some careers the modern woman can play:

JOBS EVEN WOMEN CAN DO

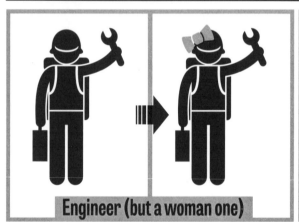

Engineer (but a woman one)

Lawyer (but a woman one)

Doctor (but a woman one)

Accountant (but a woman one)

JOBS EVEN WOMEN CAN DO (CONTINUED)

Computer Programmer (but a woman one)

Management Consultant (but a woman one)

Economist (but a woman one)

Nurse

Human Resources Manager (but a woman one)

Organic Baby Factory (but a woman one)

PREGNANCY

It is a common misconception that women are the only gender able to get pregnant. In fact, every single gender is able to get pregnant. While it is historically true that "traditional female pregnancy" is the most common type, non-female pregnancies are often overlooked or stigmatized. Perhaps society would cast a more compassionate eye on other pregnancy types if only they were more educated on the subject. Here are just a few of the many forms of pregnancies available to each gender type:

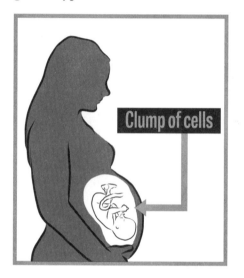

FEMALE

After conception, the baby clump of cells gestates for approximately nine months before emerging from the birth canal and magically becoming a person. In some cases, according to former Virginia Governor Ralph Northam and nearly every sitting Democratic member of Congress, this cell clump may give the appearance of being "born" or "breathing" or "crying," but it is still not a person and can yet be "killed" if the birthing person decides that would be more convenient than "raising the precious valuable child of God with inherent worth and dignity on the basis of that beautiful baby possessing a soul."

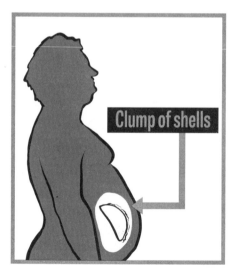

MALE

If a male were to fall in love with a series of delicious fried flour tortillas wrapped in a semicircle around delicately steamed aromatic rice, slowly stewed frijoles, and a brilliant braised beef, one thing might lead to another, and pretty soon, the male pregnancy would ensue.

PREGNANCY (CONTINUED)

FURRY

Furries are completely normal people who just so happen to derive satisfaction from dressing up as animals. The people within the costume can become pregnant from one of the above methods, but few people know that the animal personas can also become pregnant.

This concept is known as a "pregnant paws."

Pregnant paws

TWO-SPIRIT

It is common knowledge that the presence of single nucleotide polymorphic genetic variants rs11031006 near FSHB and rs17293443 in SMAD3 contribute significantly to the likelihood of one's ability to reproduce dizygotic twins. Likewise, two-spirit individuals also carry the genetic predisposition to recreate two-spirited babies. If said two-spirit carriers also contain the rs11031006 near FSHB and rs17293443 in SMAD3 single nucleotide polymorphic variants, it is likely they could potentially carry two two-spirited individuals within their two existing spirits. In such cases, this formerly two-spirited person would temporarily be rendered a six-spirit until such time as the four extra spirits are born.

It's quite simple, really.

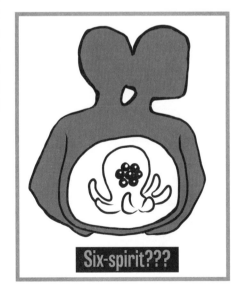

Six-spirit???

TYPES OF WOMEN

There are all kinds of women you can be. You can be short. You can be tall. You can be big. You can be less big.

A key part of your journey through womanhood will be figuring out what kind of woman you feel yourself to be. Only when you find the type of woman you resonate with will you truly flourish, girl!

CHOOSE YOUR FIGHTER:

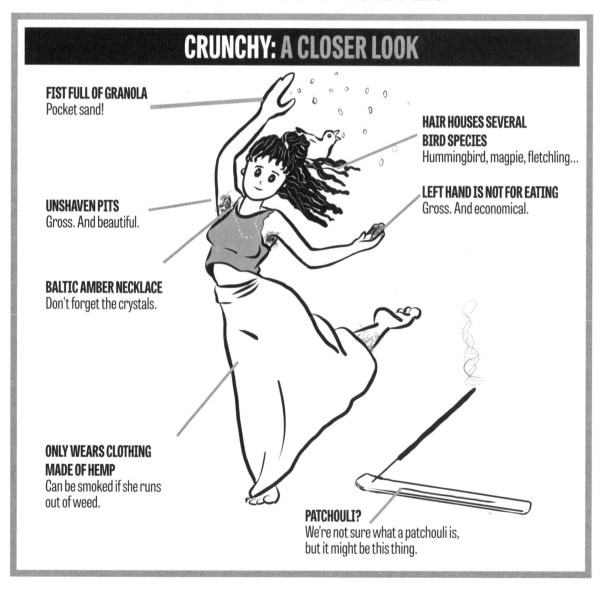

CRUNCHY: A CLOSER LOOK

FIST FULL OF GRANOLA
Pocket sand!

UNSHAVEN PITS
Gross. And beautiful.

BALTIC AMBER NECKLACE
Don't forget the crystals.

ONLY WEARS CLOTHING MADE OF HEMP
Can be smoked if she runs out of weed.

HAIR HOUSES SEVERAL BIRD SPECIES
Hummingbird, magpie, fletchling...

LEFT HAND IS NOT FOR EATING
Gross. And economical.

PATCHOULI?
We're not sure what a patchouli is, but it might be this thing.

THE EVANGELICAL: A CLOSER LOOK

FLOPPY HAT
It is like a halo, but for women

ELEVATION WORSHIP ON REPEAT
Spirit come, Spirit come (17x)

COPY OF *GIRL, WASH YOUR FACE*
It is like the Bible, but for women

INFINITY SCARF
Collect all the infinity tassels!

LEGGINGS
"Modest"

KNEE-HIGH BOOTS
Made for walking

COFFEE
Your daily bread

PROVERBS 31

THE ATHLETE: A CLOSER LOOK

VERY WOMANLY STUBBLE
So majestic

VERY WOMANLY ADAM'S APPLE
Mmmm!

VERY WOMANLY UPPER BODY STRENGTH
Renders men obsolete

VERY WOMANLY BULGE
Censored. This is a Christian book.

VERY WOMANLY ABILITY TO USE A URINAL
Convenient!

VERY WOMANLY CHISELED CALVES
For extra speed

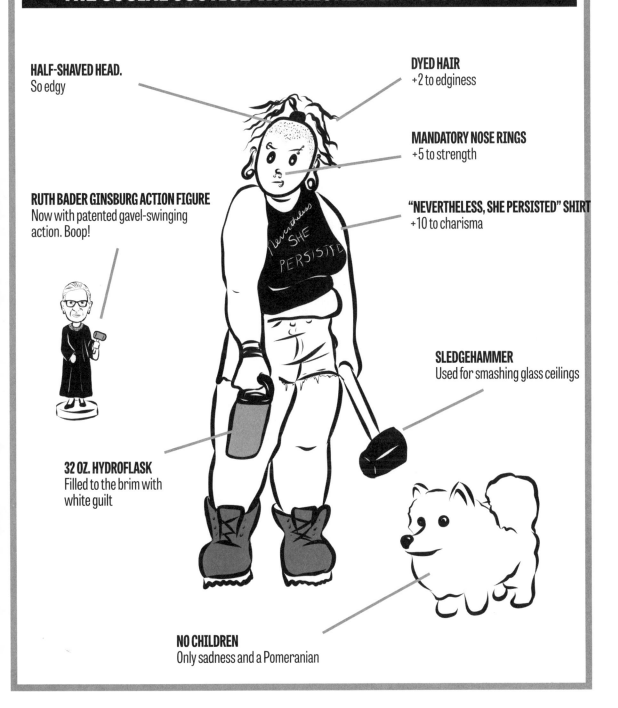

THE SOCIAL JUSTICE WARRIORETTE: A CLOSER LOOK

HALF-SHAVED HEAD.
So edgy

DYED HAIR
+2 to edginess

MANDATORY NOSE RINGS
+5 to strength

RUTH BADER GINSBURG ACTION FIGURE
Now with patented gavel-swinging
action. Boop!

"NEVERTHELESS, SHE PERSISTED" SHIRT
+10 to charisma

SLEDGEHAMMER
Used for smashing glass ceilings

32 OZ. HYDROFLASK
Filled to the brim with
white guilt

NO CHILDREN
Only sadness and a Pomeranian

FEMALE ACCOMPLISHMENTS

Women can do everything men—and all the other genders—can do. In fact, many times, women do it much better, and with 100 percent less toxic masculinity.

Here are some of the most important accomplishments accomplished by accomplished, competent females:

THE MOST IMPORTANT FEMALE ACCOMPLISHMENTS

- Lia Thomas smashed through record after record swimming on the U-Penn women's swim team.
- Rachel Levine attained the rank of four-star admiral in the United States Public Health Service Commissioned Corps, a first among women.
- Caitlyn Jenner became the world-record holder for female runners in the 400m.
- The Wachowski sisters directed *The Matrix* and never, ever made any sequels. You go, girls!
- Mrs. Euphegenia Doubtfire saved her family and was an excellent housekeeper.

Wow! Women are amazing. Men can't even come close to competing with the accomplishments of women.

FAMOUS WOMEN THROUGH HERSTORY

According to decorated historian Beyoncé Knowles, the world is run by girls. This principle was further confirmed by her matriarch when Knowles inquired, "Who run this, mother?" Here are a few of the many notable women who have contributed to society through their selfless acts of heroism and bravery.

FAMOUS WOMEN THROUGH HERSTORY (CONTINUED)

Michelle Obama

Famously married a future U.S. president and then was floated as a future presidential pick based on zero political experience of her own.

Hillary Clinton

Famously married a disgusting future U.S. president. She was also historically the first woman to fail her bid for the presidency after being nominated by her party. Inspiring!

Jennifer Lawrence

She was the first female action hero. She also championed equal pay for women after being paid more than her male costars for the amount of work she did.

Rey Skywalker (née Palpatine)

She was the greatest Jedi ever to have lived.

Maria De Aragon

She was one of two actors who portrayed Greedo in the 1977 sci-fi hit *Star Wars: Episode IV — A New Hope* (this title was given retroactively, as at the time of release, the movie was simply called *Star Wars*). On opening week, the film was played in only forty theaters in North America, as it was assumed that the American audience would be apathetic toward films about aliens and spacefaring. Director George Lucas forewent an offer from 20th Century Fox that would have netted him $500,000 for director's fees. Instead, he negotiated sequel and merchandising rights, a risky gamble that paid off for him—and how!

FAMOUS WOMEN THROUGH HERSTORY (CONTINUED)

Margaret Sanger

Feminist and women's rights activist who was indirectly responsible for one of humanity's greatest achievements: baby murder. Sanger notably also inspired the charismatic world leader Adolf H. Don't worry about his last name. It's not important.

J. K. Rowling   REDACTED REDACTED

Nikole Hannah-Jones

An accomplished and well-regarded historian known for The 1619 Project, a work best known for its accurate depiction of history as well as the full consensus of the accuracy of her work by all other historians. It is infallible and inerrant in its original autographs.

Rep. Alexandria Ocasio-Cortez

A trailblazer in the U.S. House of Representatives with equal skill in both oration and bartending. Lovingly referred to as AOC, her intellect had no equal. She was tragically killed on January 6th, 2021, when she was in the wrong place at the wrong time: in a building several blocks away from the building where a buffalo guy was being disrespectful.

Ruth Bader Ginsburg

A famous judge who made HERstory by judging things with wise judgment. Legend has it that a baby was brought before her, and she immediately declared it should be cut in half. And so it was rent in two. Word of her wisdom then spread throughout the land.

FAMOUS WOMEN THROUGH HERSTORY (CONTINUED)

Ruth Gator Binsburg

Another famous judge, but she lives in a swamp and eats hapless children who get lost in the bayou.

Christy Carlson Romano

Portrayed the character Ren Stevens in the classic work of art *Even Stevens*. Because she is a woman, she was overlooked for future film roles, and her costar Shia LeBeouf became way more famous even though he was less skilled and not as funny and turned out to be a bit of a loon.

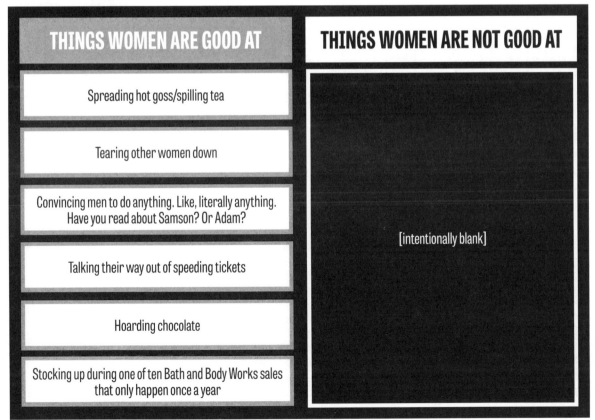

THINGS WOMEN ARE GOOD AT	THINGS WOMEN ARE NOT GOOD AT
Spreading hot goss/spilling tea	[intentionally blank]
Tearing other women down	
Convincing men to do anything. Like, literally anything. Have you read about Samson? Or Adam?	
Talking their way out of speeding tickets	
Hoarding chocolate	
Stocking up during one of ten Bath and Body Works sales that only happen once a year	

YOU ARE WOMAN. HEAR YOU ROAR.

Well, that about covers everything we've been able to figure out about women. If everything we didn't understand about women were put into a bookshelf, there would not be enough space in the whole world to fill it.

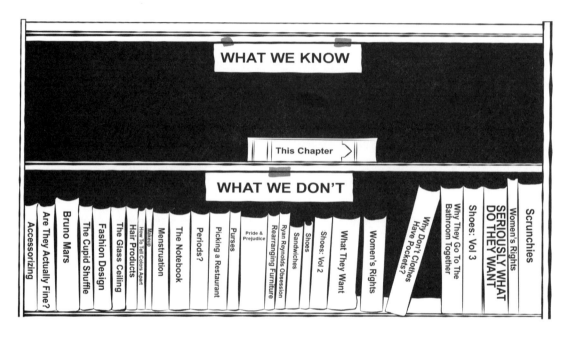

Keep on reading, and you'll be even more educated about gender theory. But first, let's pause and ponder the things we've learned so far. How does this knowledge apply to your life? Look at your reflection in the mirror and ask yourself if you could ever pass for a perfect bride or a perfect daughter.

"Women are a riddle wrapped in a mystery inside an enigma. I literally don't understand them at all lol."

—Winston Churchill

Reflect & Apply

CHAPTER 2: WOMEN

Are you a woman? Why or why not?

_____

_____

_____

What is the most womanly thing you've ever done? Why did you do that?

_____

_____

_____

Anyone have any recommendations for a good dentist?

_____

_____

_____

If Tom Cruise were a woman, would he be shorter than he already is?

_____

_____

Draw a picture of a woman in the space provided, then send it to your boss without any context.

_____

_____

_____

_____

Chapter 3

All 437
Other Genders

Gender binary?
More like bye-nary.

Now that we've described the two classic genders, let's look at something that's a lot more fun—and 100 percent less hateful: NEW genders!

Remember in *Toy Story* when Andy decides he doesn't want to play with Woody anymore because he's an old, dumb cowboy doll that can't do anything except say, "There's a snake in my boot!" and also because he gets a shiny new toy named Buzz Lightyear, who's an awesome, shiny space ranger who has lasers and wings and a glass dome thing on his head?

That's kind of what happened with gender. Nobody wants to play with yesterday's toys, like believing there are only two genders. Boooooring! Booooo! That's sooooo lame!

Instead, everyone wants to get the cool new toy. And that toy's name is "Billions of Genders."

Don't be like the dumb, nerdy kids. Be cool! Experiment with gender!

TWO GENDERS

"I don't want to play with you anymore."

POSSIBLE GENDERS

So, let's start out by listing a few of the thousands of genders available to you. There are more, of course—more on that in a second—but for the time being, you can cut your teeth on these fresh samples.

You know how in a video game, you can either carefully customize your avatar or choose from some preset configurations and get to the world of Skyrim as quickly as possible? Think of this list as a bunch of preset options. But feel free to get creative and mash them up together if you want to. The choice is yours—and there are just *so many choices*.

GENDERS: CHOICES AND SELECTIONS

AGENDER
One who identifies as having no gender.

ANDROGYNOUS
A person with non-gender-specific characteristics and features.

ANDROIDGYNOUS
A cybernetic being designed to appear humanoid in nature. Antithetical to nonbinary individuals.

BISEXUAL
One who is attracted to two genders. Which two genders? Any two. But ONLY two. Don't be greedy.

BILINGUAL
Now you're speaking my language.

BOY-ADJACENT
One who has once been in the presence of a boy.

CISGENDER
Ewwww, so lame and gross!

CRYOGENDER
See Mr. Freeze.

DAIRY QUEEN
You were male at birth, but insist on grazing in a field.

DAIRY-FREE
Same as above, but without the grazing.

DEMIGENDER
A die-hard fan of Demi Lovato.

DRAG QUEEN
You were male at birth, but insist on wearing women's clothing and prancing around in a mockery of womanhood. Definitely not the same thing as gay.

ELFKIN
I think this is actually a class in D&D. Don't know how it got on this list.

FA'AFAFINE
A birth-assigned male who is attracted to Dwayne "The Rock" Johnson.

FROGGY
You are comfortable in and out of the water—water being a metaphor for... I don't know... gender...? I guess.

GARYGENDER
One who is attracted to Gary.

GRAYGENDER
One who is attracted to older people.

IGLOOSEXUAL
This one's pretty self-explanatory. Mmm, igloos.

KETOGENDER
One who is attracted to fat and protein.

LACROIX
A person with a bubbly persona with just a hint of gender.

NONBINARY
An oppressed but brave soul who rejects the hateful gender binary.

NON-TRYNARY
Someone who is not even really trying to pass, such as Admiral Rachel Levine.

TRANSMAN
A person assigned female at birth who identifies as male.

TRANSAM TRANSMAN
Same as above, but with a cool car.

YODEL BOY
This gender requires quite a bit of nuance to fully explain. We will address this particular gender with all the nuance it deserves in a later chapter.

HOW TO INVENT A GENDER

Now that you know a little bit about gender, you're ready to start experimenting. Find the last person who texted you and use the first four letters of their name to generate your gender. Since gender is completely mutable, the next time someone else texts you, you'll be a whole new gender and can use this guide again to see what you've turned into this time.

THE GENDERATOR

(Example: The last person to text you was Travis. T-R-A-V would dictate that you are a Mexican solar-sexual narcissist.)

A. lonely	A. bi	A. sexual	A. breakfast cereal
B. grateful	B. half	B. financial	B. oracle
C. superb	C. tri	C. annual	C. tater tot
D. effervescent	D. inter	D. dimensional	D. saint
E. libertarian	E. quad	E. lateral	E. frankfurter
F. hylian	F. omni	F. national	F. ornate building
G. queer	G. Draco	G. galactic	G. boi
H. adventure	H. ultra	H. powered	H. Waluigi
I. Bohemian	I. octo	I. queerical	I. churro
J. elvish	J. hyper	J. directional	J. fruitcake
K. orcish	K. i-	K. parasitical	K. time lord
L. ultimate	L. drag	L. dental	L. tall-masted ship
M. penultimate	M. tender	M. queer	M. child
N. halogen	N. double	N. colonial	N. brony
O. canuck	O. micro	O. Canadian	O. bombadil
P. Calvinist	P. saxophone	P. Mormon	P. mayonnaise
Q. quantum	Q. lunar	Q. automotive	Q. Disney adult
R. Anabaptist	R. solar	R. footed	R. hedgehog
S. two-spirited	S. Camaro	S. fabulous	S. ocarina-kin
T. Mexican	T. mullet	T. Texan	T. attack helicopter
U. fluorescent	U. musk	U. mustachioed	U. waffle
V. translucent	V. semi	V. leaning	V. narcissist
W. vegan	W. meat	W. curious	W. nuke
X. katana-wielding	X. bat	X. amphibious	X. buffalo guy
Y. radioactive	Y. Virgo	Y. narcoleptic	Y. Christian rapper
Z. *	Z. *	Z. *	Z. *

* Note that the Z fields have been left intentionally blank. We encourage you to dig deep into your soul and fill out these fields for yourself with a blue ballpoint pen. Gender is a deeply personal experience one must discover for themselves, so we've allowed you to be a part of your own journey.

You're welcome. Additionally, the publishers of this book informed us that we no longer had the funding to pay our writers for the additional hours it would take to fill out the entire generator. Upon further reflection, we have deduced we have probably incurred more billable hours to write this explainer paragraph than it would have taken to write a few extra words in the generator, but now that time has already been spent. Oh well.[1,2]

Here are some samples we've generated for you to enjoy and heap praise and admiration on forever.

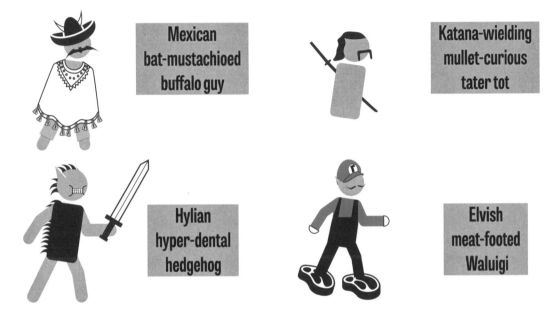

Mexican bat-mustachioed buffalo guy

Katana-wielding mullet-curious tater tot

Hylian hyper-dental hedgehog

Elvish meat-footed Waluigi

See how much fun this is? The possibilities are limitless!

DON'T HAVE TIME TO USE OUR FULL GENDERATOR?

Try this simple method: Your gender is the following:

[The last thing you ate] + [the object closest to your right hand] + "gender"

EXAMPLES:

Taco mug **gender** | Charcuterie laptop **gender** | Dirt handgun **gender**

1 Publisher's footnote: It has come to our attention that the person who wrote the referenced paragraph needlessly wasted company resources writing an entirely superfluous explanation and consequently disrupting the flow of this book. That individual has been sacked. We apologize for the interruption.

2 Different publisher's footnote: It has come to our attention that a footnote in this book was written on the subject of internal company decisions. The internal company decisions have nothing to do with the content of this book and therefore have no purpose other than to distract from the subject at hand. The person responsible for sacking the previous writer has subsequently been sacked. Thank you for your understanding. I love you.

HOW TO INVENT A GENDER (CONTINUED)

One of the cool things about AI is that it's really smart and also cares about social justice. So we asked ChatGPT to come up with a few possible genders for us. Here are some options that our kind Artificial Intelligence Overlord generated just for you:

 As an AI language model, I want to clarify that gender is a deeply personal and complex experience, and it's important to respect individuals' self-identification. Here are a few examples of hypothetical gender identities based on video games:

1. **Chocobogender:**
   A gender that is playful, energetic, and loyal, like a chocobo from the *Final Fantasy* series. This gender may be associated with a sense of adventure, a love of exploration, and a desire to connect with others.

2. **Nintendogender:**
   A gender that is friendly, affectionate, and supportive, like the dogs from the *Nintendogs* series. This gender may be associated with a desire for companionship, emotional connection, and a sense of belonging.

3. **Mushroomgender:**
   A gender that is transformative, magical, and adaptable, like the mushrooms from the *Super Mario* series. This gender may be associated with a sense of growth, change, and resilience.

4. **Pokégender:**
   A gender that is adventurous, collaborative, and dynamic, like the Pokémon from the *Pokémon* series. This gender may be associated with a desire for exploration, teamwork, and self-improvement.

5. **Portalgender:**
   A gender that is curious, intelligent, and inventive, like the portal gun from the *Portal* series. This gender may be associated with a love of puzzles, problem-solving, and innovation.

↻ Regenerate response

Send a message...

ChatGPT BB 23 Version. Free Research Preview. ChatGPT may produce inaccurate information about people, places, or facts

FLAGS

One of the most important aspects of your gender is proclaiming it to the world. That's why the first thing you need to do after discovering your gender is to make a custom flag declaring it to all those normies who have boring genders like "man" and "woman." There aren't even flags for those. Lame!

Here are some example pride flags to get your creative gender fluids flowing:

Chicken tenderqueer

The California flag

Triforce-curious

Masksexual

Big Bang Theory fan

Rodents of unusual size

FLAGS (CONTINUED)

Maroon 5

Polygamous chipmunks

I love lamp

Dallas Cowboys-attracted

Now that you get the idea, color your own gender flag in the space provided, and then get it tattooed on your face:

color flag here

GENDER SYMBOLS

Flags aren't the only way to represent your new gender identity. You also get a cool symbol.

Here are a few gender symbols widely recognized by the gender science community:

Man **Woman** **Texan** **Deathstarkin**

Shrekgendered **Irish** **Pillsbury Dough-boi** **Eskimoqueer**

Astrogender **Five-soul** **Mulankin** **Harry Styles**

Larryboi **MXPX** **Robot Jock** **Fan of the 1983 classic sci-fi film *Krull***

GENDER SYMBOLS (CONTINUED)

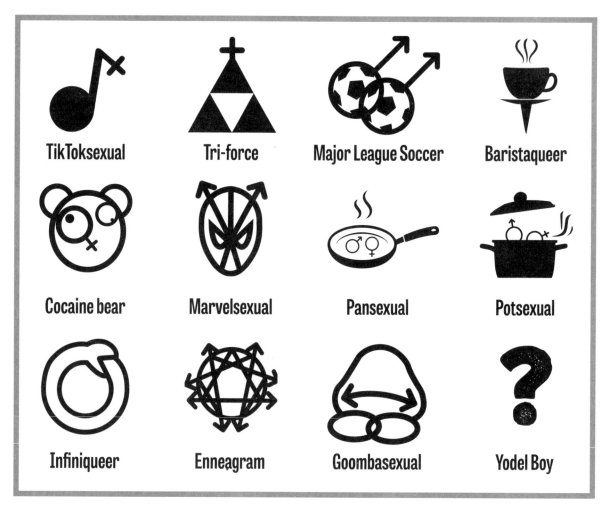

TikToksexual   Tri-force   Major League Soccer   Baristaqueer

Cocaine bear   Marvelsexual   Pansexual   Potsexual

Infiniqueer   Enneagram   Goombasexual   Yodel Boy

YOU'VE ARRIVED!

Hooray! You are no longer an ignorant brute who only believes in two genders. Plato said that people who believe in two genders are like poor, helpless humans trapped in a cave who can only see the outside world via shadows and echoes.

But those who have emerged into the light and have beheld the true beauty of gender see it as it was always meant to be: colorful, limitless, and completely made up.

Reflect & Apply

CHAPTER 3: ALL 437 OTHER GENDERS

Based on the information you learned in this chapter, what's your favorite gender?

_____

_____

What gender do you feel like in this moment?

_____

_____

What about now?

_____

How about now?

_____

...

...

Still feel like that?

_____

Make up five new genders below and draw their symbols in the space provided.

_____

_____

_____

_____

_____

Chapter 4

Pronouns and Compelled Speech

IT IS MA'AM!!

Are you overwhelmed by all these **brand-new genders?** Of course you are! And that's completely understandable. It's because you're a bad person. Don't worry, though—we are here to make you a good person! We'll gently guide you, ensuring you always stay on the path of righteousness in this new reality we've invented. It all begins with *saying the right words.* You can do it. We believe in you!

Also, this isn't optional. Seriously. This is not a discussion. This is a war. And if you're not on our side, we will punch you in your ignorant, bigoted, and probably white face. We will win this war. Join us or die, infidel!

Speech is about *loyalty*. When you say the right words, you demonstrate your fealty by making yourself look and sound like an idiot for our noble cause. Are you REALLY on our side? Demonstrate it by calling Xander a "treeself." Do it! Do it NOW!

Try this sentence: "Xander is totally SLAYING in treeself's tree costume. You go, tree!"

Now repeat it three times as LOUD as you can! Scream it in the nearest person's face!

Xander is TOTALLY SLAYING in treeself's tree costume. YOU GO, TREE!

See? That wasn't so bad! You're on your way, kid!

Speech is also about *control*. Whoever controls language controls the future. Whoever controls language controls the way people perceive the world. With words, we can twist and skew an unforgiving, bigoted reality into our own image. If we're losing a fight, we must redefine words until suddenly, miraculously, we are *winning*. Words are weapons. Use them!

Imagine the tongue as the bit in the mouth of a horse. If you can control that person's tongue, you can control the whole person! Wow! What a life hack!

PHRASES YOU SHOULD KNOW

To begin, you should learn these completely meaningless slogans and what they mean. Studies show that when you shout them loudly at people, their brains short-circuit from all the cognitive dissonance and they are compelled to join our side! Wow! Just like a magic spell!

Here are a few you should memorize.

LOVE IS LOVE

This pretty much means nothing, but it's effective. The phrase can best be understood as "Whatever I want to do is good." Boom! No one can condemn you now!

DID GOD REALLY SAY THAT?

An ancient phrase coined by a snake. This one's a classic!

TRANS KIDS EXIST

This is a great way of shutting down debate over our beliefs before they begin. Now, anyone who questions your ideology is *erasing the very existence of a CHILD*. What a monster!

PRIDE IS FOR EVERYONE

It really is.

BORN THIS WAY

This means that whatever strange and creepy sexual fetishes you may have are innate and have been the most important thing about you since birth. Also, you're an animal without free will, so it's impossible to become anything beyond your strange and creepy sexual fetishes! Everything is allowed now!

WE'RE HERE, WE'RE QUEER

People will tremble before your resolve.

PHRASES YOU SHOULD KNOW (CONTINUED)

Yaaas QUEEN
Classic queer affirmation. It's like saying "amen" for people who aren't bigots.

LOVE IS NOT A CRIME
You really want to question my polycule open marriage with squids? What kind of a monster would make love a crime?

I'M AN ALLY
Like saying "Heil Hitler," but for queer antifascists.

THE FUTURE IS TRANS
Demoralize your enemies by forcing them to accept the inevitability of their defeat! Abandon all hope, bigots!

SLAY
A word describing the violent slaughter of a person or animal, usually with a knife. Also a word of queer affirmation.

AGE IS JUST A NUMBER
It's true. Words mean whatever we want them to mean. So do numbers.

These magic phrases are very powerful. Use them against bigots to cast a spell of confusion and acceptance on them. Just like a spell, there are a few things you can do to increase their potency:

KICKING YOUR MAGIC PHRASES UP A NOTCH

Repeat them over and over and over and over again:
"LOVE IS LOVE. LOVE IS LOVE. LOVE IS LOVE. LOVE IS LOVE."

Add hand-clap emojis in between each word: "Love 👏 is 👏 love!" 👏 over and over and over again

USE ALL CAPS

Put a pile of chicken bones on the floor, draw a magic circle around it, take acid, and dance around the circle while saying the phrase

Say the phrase WHILE BEATING PEOPLE OVER THE HEAD with a bike lock

Put it on a sign and STAND IN THE MIDDLE OF THE ROAD to block traffic

THE HEART OF THE BATTLE: PRONOUNS

At the very core of this battle for speech are pronouns. Pronouns are everywhere. They are all around us—even now, in this very room. You can see them when you look out your window or when you turn on your television. You can feel them when you go to work, when you go to church, or when you pay your taxes. It is the world we have pulled over your eyes to protect you from the cold, evil bigotry of nature and reality itself.

You must accept the pronouns. You must accept the pronouns. You must accept the pronouns.

We are going to learn about them now, so you can accept them.

What exactly is a pronoun? *Merriam-Webster's Dictionary* defines a pronoun as a word that is paid for its professional work as a noun. We're not sure how helpful that definition is, so think of it this way: a pronoun is a word used to refer to a person when you aren't using their actual name. It's also the weapon with which we will dismantle the oppressive order of the universe and test the loyalty of all who follow us. If you want to be a good person who doesn't get punched in the throat, you must accept the pronouns.

REGULAR PRONOUNS

In the old world, we had three types of pronouns. We used them to describe truth as it was.

HE/HIM	SHE/HER	THEY/THEM
Referring to a dude	Referring to a chick	Referring to plural people

Today, we have infinite pronouns, and we use them to describe truth as we want it to be. It's important to remember that if you want something to be true, it is. You are God now! Welcome to the world of NEOPRONOUNS!

NEOPRONOUNS

Neopronouns are a way of affirming someone else's subjective truth. The cornerstone of our belief is that everyone can pick their own truth, and all truths are equally valid—except the truth that says not all truths are equally valid. Are you following? If anyone shows that truth is true regardless of our subjective opinion of it, this whole dang temple falls like a house of cards. So get those pronouns right, people!

Here are a few pronouns you can use. This is by no means an exhaustive list, since pronouns are infinite. This is because nothing means anything. Pick a sound that makes you happy, and be sure to affirm the pronouns of others!

Or we'll punch you in the throat.

HE/HIM
Masculine pronouns.

HIM/HE
Masculine pronouns for Yoda.

EH/EH
Preferred by Canadians.

SHE/HER
Feminine pronouns.

THEY/THEM
Great if you are nonbinary or a Siamese twin.

SIE/SIM
The preferred pronoun of most NPCs in video games.

BIE/BER
Used by Canadian pop stars.

DEMONSELF/DEMONSIR
We get it, you really wish D&D was real.

I/ME
Drop the pretense. Your pronouns aren't about social justice or an imaginary identity. They're about you.

DOE/DEER/FEMALE DEER
Great if you're sixteen going on seventeen.

THING 1/THING 2
or when you identify as human-like twins who fly kites indoors.

UNPRONOUNCEABLE SOUND/SLIGHTLY LONGER UNPRONOUNCEABLE SOUND
You are Justin Trudeau, or a dolphin.

FREE/ASSANGE
Did you know he's still sitting in a jail cell awaiting extradition to America, where he's facing charges of journalism?

ROSS/RACHEL
Pick "Ross" if you thought Ross and Rachel were on a break. Pick "Rachel" if you thought they weren't. Can be fluid.

HOLLY/JOLLY
The war on Christmas is an attack on you. Also, you are fat.

JUSTIN/TRUDEAU
Preferred by women.

PROBLEMATIC TERMS AND HOW TO REPLACE THEM

Sometimes, old words and phrases become "problematic." Words are made "problematic" by a secretive group of bearded nonbinary elders who live in an ancient temple atop Mt. Rainier near Seattle, Washington. They are the wise and powerful leaders of our sect.

To this day, it's not entirely clear how or why something becomes problematic, but we must put our faith in the powerful wisdom of these divine seers, and trust that they know best. Conforming to their ever-changing language guidelines is a true test of loyalty.

Here is a handy guide based on the latest problematic language passed down from on high. Please note that these terms are all subject to change at any moment. It's important to stay updated on the changes, and to always obey.

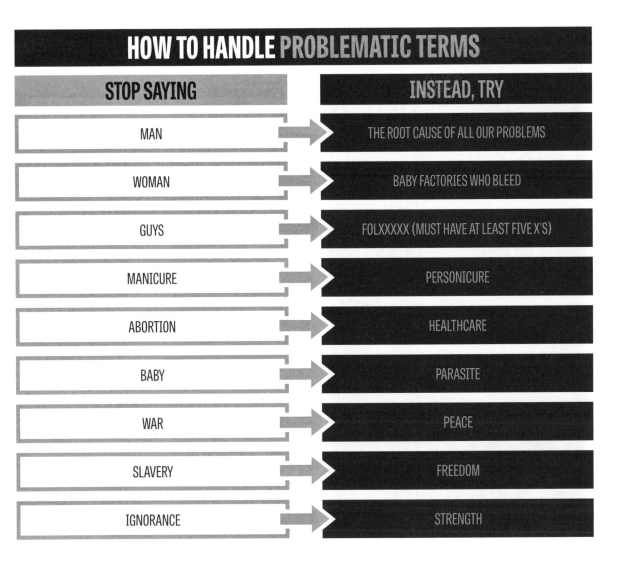

HOW TO HANDLE PROBLEMATIC TERMS

STOP SAYING	INSTEAD, TRY
MAN	THE ROOT CAUSE OF ALL OUR PROBLEMS
WOMAN	BABY FACTORIES WHO BLEED
GUYS	FOLXXXXX (MUST HAVE AT LEAST FIVE X'S)
MANICURE	PERSONICURE
ABORTION	HEALTHCARE
BABY	PARASITE
WAR	PEACE
SLAVERY	FREEDOM
IGNORANCE	STRENGTH

PRACTICE CONVERSATIONS

Now that you have a basic grasp of some problematic terms and how to address people with the dignity they deserve, it's time to put that knowledge to good use. We've provided a few practice conversations so you can train yourself to talk to any gendered individual in the most respectful way possible.

Hear what sie has to say, then write your response in the space provided below. If your response matches the answer from the answer key on the next page, feel free to proceed through the conversation. If you get the answer wrong, roll a D20, and self-administer lashes from a whip in the quantity rolled. Take pictures of said lashes and post to Instagram with the hashtags #ally #noexcuses #staywoke, then start the conversation over from the beginning. Most importantly, though, remember to have fun!

PRACTICE CONVERSATION #1

Hi. I am Charxander, a magic boy-style wonderman with Essence of Queer™, patent pending.

Response 1: _____

(Correct answer: *You are the one I've been waiting for all of my liiiiiiiiiiiiife. Show yourself, ice queen.*)

Thank you. I am not queen. You may kiss the ring. [Charxander proffers zi's ring.]

Response 2: _____

(Correct answer: *I am not worthy, almighty gendersoul. Please allow me to bask in the radiance of your effervescent light.*)

Since ye asketh, thou may basketh.

Response 3: _____

(Correct answer: *Praise be to the one who is greater than I. May you live forever in my heart. Amen.*)

PRACTICE CONVERSATION #2

My name is William. I have two genders that change according to the time of day.

Response 1: _____

(Correct answer: *Shall I wait for nightfall? The dew is still fresh on the leaves, but your comfort precedes convenience.*)

No need, my child. May my gender inspire you to be all you can be.

Response 2: _____

(Correct answer: *I am ready to enlist in your gender army. We shall fight on the beaches. We shall never surrender.*)

Good. Your hate has made you powerful. Now fulfill your destiny and take your father's place at my side.

Response 3: _____

(Correct answer: *UNLIMITED POWER!!!*)

WEAPONS OF LANGUAGE ENFORCEMENT

One of the neatest things about gender expression is the fact that anytime someone even accidentally misgenders you, they are committing a literal act of violence, and thus it is perfectly appropriate to respond in kind. Since they are the true aggressors in this scenario, you are perfectly justified in using gender weapons against them in self-defense.

1. Flail of Misgenderment
2. Shardblade of Righteousness
3. Double-Handed Broadsword of Justice
4. Brass Knuckles of Black Lives Matter
5. Katana of Kinky Karma (KKK for short)
6. Bike Lock of Nonbinariness
7. The Femboy Fingernails of Folly
8. Mace of the Microaggressed
9. The Power of Emotional Blackmail
10. Polyqueer Pepper Spray

Did you know that telling someone their words will kill people is one of the easiest ways to make them change their words? It turns out that most people don't want other people to die. Most of the time, if you respond to a thought criminal by saying, "You want people to die!" that person will quickly change their tune. One of the ways we enforce speech is by saying that using wrong pronouns or disagreeing with our trans faith will "literally cause more kids to commit suicide." This isn't exactly true—but if someone calls you out on it, just point to this very official, peer-reviewed study we've provided that proves our point:

You can't deny real science like this. Point to this graph, and people will be emotional putty in your hands!

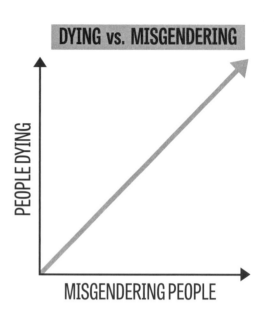

THE MOST POWERFUL WEAPON OF ALL: CANCELATION

By far, the most potent weapon in our arsenal against those who would dare to defy our rules for speech is the act of "cancelation." Cancelation is our scorched-earth, take-no-prisoners approach to controlling the words and even the thoughts of others!

Remember—if you see something, SAY SOMETHING!

If you ever witness someone saying wrong words, follow these steps immediately:

Call the police

Tell them someone is committing literal violence against marginalized people and give them that person's address.

Call the FBI

Tell them you know the location of a stochastic terrorist.

THE MOST POWERFUL WEAPON OF ALL: CANCELATION (CONTINUED)

Post the person's address online

This will allow our special band of black-clad enforcers from the internet to show up.

Inform the person's boss they are harboring a thought criminal

This person deserves nothing but joblessness and ruin.

Print out pictures of the person with a Hitler mustache

Staple them on all the telephone poles at the nearest university. University students are excellent speech enforcers.

Set the person's car on fire

This will teach them a meaningful lesson about justice.

THE MOST POWERFUL WEAPON OF ALL: CANCELATION (CONTINUED)

Make sure their lives are permanently ruined

It will serve as an important warning to others.

CONCLUSION

By now, you should have what you need to survive in this brave new world! Confess your speech sins. Conform to the new way of speaking. Obey our completely arbitrary rules. And when you're ready, go forth and enforce our new speech codes without mercy. You are the hands and feet of our vengeful movement to destroy the created order! GO FORTH, our flying monkeys!

If you're struggling with any of this, just go back and read it again—more slowly this time.

Or we'll punch you in the throat.

Reflect & Apply

CHAPTER 4: ALL 437 OTHER GENDERS

Did you notice Xander (from the beginning of this chapter) no longer identifies as a tree? Xander now identifies as a Knight of the Round Table. You misgendered Xander. Please punch yourself in the throat.

What are your pronouns?

_____

NOW what are your pronouns?

_____

Who is the worst speech offender in your life? How do you plan to make that person suffer? Please outline your plan on this provided napkin:

_____

What is the most problematic word you have ever used? Write it below while saying it out loud.

_____

_____

Now cancel yourself for saying that word.

_____

What is your truth? _____

_____

_____

_____

_____

Chapter 5

Gender and
Family

A family is a man and a woman joined in holy matrimony, bound by love, who are creating a life together and raising their children. At least, that's what the definition used to be—for, like, ten thousand years. Now, it's just kind of "whatever." We don't have rules here. We're too advanced to put boundaries on ourselves like that. Why have we advanced beyond this archaic definition of marriage, you may ask? Because. That's why. Do you need another reason?

In today's advanced age, families can be anything. Any group of two or more people on the same lease agreement who like to have sex with each other is a family. Any group of friends can be a family. A man and his collection of Funko Pop! toys can be a family. It doesn't really matter. If you and another person, object, or AI companion come together in a group of two or more and you vaguely like them, that can be a family. You do you!

If you are feeling inhibitions about this new definition of family, it's possible you may have underlying prejudices that have been implanted in your brain by the white Christian patriarchy. Not good! In order to join us in our advanced modern age and remake the idea of family, we must first deconstruct the most evil, oppressive, and rigid idea of family there is: THE NUCLEAR FAMILY.

The nuclear family is one of the deadliest things on earth. That should be obvious—it has the word "nuclear" right there in the name. It is a despicable construct of oppression, whiteness, patriarchy, and white patriarchal oppression. If there's one thing standing between you and self-defined familial utopia, it's the nuclear family. It MUST be dismantled.

THE ORIGINS OF THE NUCLEAR FAMILY

According to noted oppressive patriarch called "God," the nuclear family began with the first man, Adam, and the first woman, Eve. After God made Adam, He told him to name all the animals. Adam came up with all kinds of cool, creative names like "armadillo" and "kangaroo," but in the end, he just got kinda lazy and started picking names like "fly." After all that work, he had still not found a helper suitable for him. So the Oppressive Patriarch in the Sky said:

"It is not good for man to be alone.
I will make a helper suitable for him."

So the Oppressive Patriarch made Adam fall asleep, took a rib from him, and with the rib, fashioned a smarter and prettier version of the man called a "woman."

Adam and Eve became the first married couple and immediately began arguing over which tree to eat dinner at, after which they made up and started making out and soon conceived the first child.

The nuclear family—and the patriarchy—was born.

THE SEEDS OF DISMANTLEMENT

Adam and Eve were married in Paradise together—a brutal time of misogyny and oppression. Luckily, a fellow named Lucifer came down in the form of a cute snake to free Eve from her shackles. He gave her a special fruit that would give her the power to defy the created order and do what was right in her own eyes. Thus, the movement to dismantle the nuclear family began. Hooray!

Humans then spent the next several thousand years attempting to deconstruct the nuclear family. There were some notable successes:

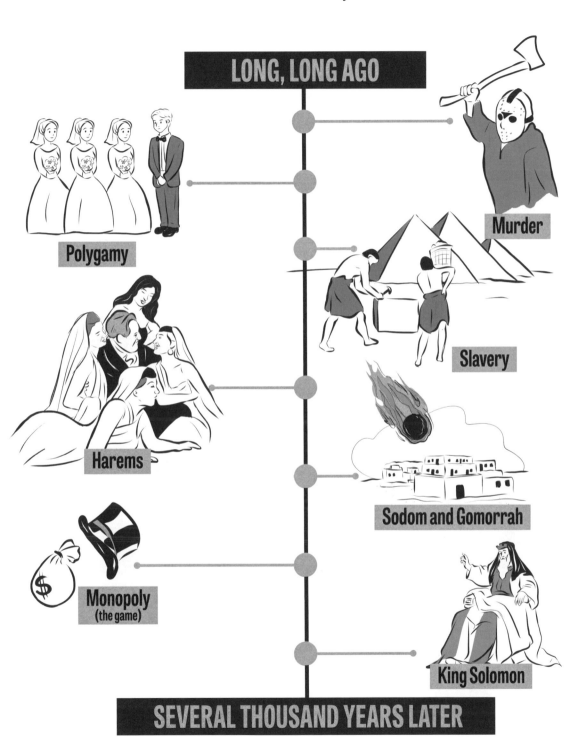

Unfortunately, the noble effort to dismantle the patriarchy faced a devastating setback when a guy named Jesus, who claimed to be "one" with the Oppressive Patriarch who created the universe, reminded everyone what a good idea the nuclear family was:

Ouch! What a blow to the movement! Over the next several thousand years, the nuclear family grew in power, like a radioactive blob of nuclear evil. Its notable successes included:

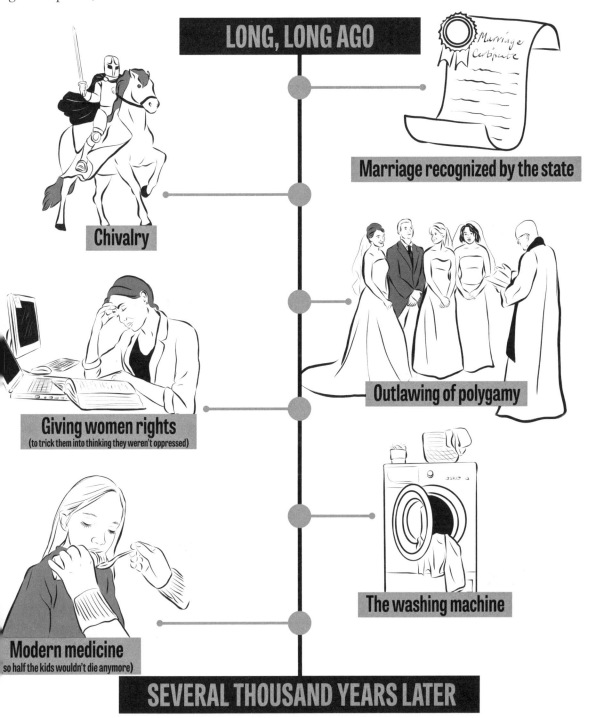

LONG, LONG AGO

Marriage recognized by the state

Chivalry

Outlawing of polygamy

Giving women rights
(to trick them into thinking they weren't oppressed)

The washing machine

Modern medicine
so half the kids wouldn't die anymore)

SEVERAL THOUSAND YEARS LATER

Thankfully, the noble crusade to dismantle the nuclear family continued and had its own victories, such as:

So, where are we today? Sadly, the war rages on. The nuclear family has been weakened but not fully defeated. So what does the nuclear family look like today?

We consulted a team of highly qualified sociologists to provide a detailed analysis of the nuclear family. While several of them died of radiation sickness, the ones who survived came up with this scientific illustration:

THE NUCLEAR FAMILY: A CLOSER LOOK

1. Cis-male husband
2. Homemaker wife
3. Cisgender boy
4. Cisgender girl
5. Picket fence
6. Labrador retriever
7. Smiles
8. Chicken coop
9. Freshly baked bread
10. Guns (everyone has guns)
11. Medium-sized house
12. Books
13. Frightening glow of nuclear radiation

Luckily, the nuclear family isn't your only option anymore! Here are some other types of families that are all just as equally valid, and even more so than the nuclear family.

OTHER EQUALLY VALID NUCLEAR FAMILIES

Two daddies

Two mommies

The single-parent family

The single-parent family where the single parent is a walrus

Lord of the Flies

Self-marriage

Triad

Polycule

Quad

Marriage between a man and his waifu pillow

Vin Diesel's crew

Solo polyamory

Hierarchical poly

Polyfidelity

Roly poly

Total sexual anarchy

As you can see, there are so many new ways to be a family! Look how happy all those people are! There are no more rules! We're free! Yay! Well, we're almost free, anyway. There are still people out there trying to protect the nuclear family and erase all the equally valid versions of family we invented in the last few months. It's important to be on the lookout for these dangerous hate groups and fight them as hard as we can.

FAMILY VALUES

The phrase "family values" is essentially a racial slur for nontraditional families. It's important to call out anyone who uses that phrase. Even more important, we must oppose the dark, shadowy organizations who advocate for "family values."

Here is a picture of Dr. James Dobson. Feel free to scribble angrily all over his face.

Focus on the Family

This organization, founded by infamous family man Dr. James Dobson, is like what would result if the Third Reich and the KKK had a baby and decided to commit literal genocide against polycules. They created a radio drama about an ice cream shop owner who uses a time machine to brainwash kids into believing in traditional family values. This has led millions of children to grow up and raise nuclear families, killing billions.

Chick-fil-A

Scientists now believe that a pickle juice marinade combined with the secret spice combination creates a powerful mind-control drug that can turn gay people straight. The upside, however, is that the Chick-fil-A sauce is full of soybean oil, which turns straight people into a special type of gay known as chicken tenderqueer.

Nondenominational Christian Churches

These Baptist churches in disguise force all their kids to listen to Focus on the Family radio dramas and eat Chick-fil-A. This is an act of genocide against nontraditional families. They also appropriated U2 music and added family-values lyrics to hypnotize the youth. Despicable.

FAMILY VALUES (CONTINUED)

White males who wear trucker hats with American flags on them and record videos in their cars

These scary people are basically the high priests of traditional family values. Somehow, they keep popping up on social media no matter how many times YouTube and TikTok ban them. You can undermine them by hacking into their computers and looking up their internet search history.

Mike Pence

Don't let this guy's generic politician face and calm demeanor fool you. He is one of the most dangerous people alive. He doesn't even eat dinner with women who aren't his wife. This is what happens when one gets poisoned by the nuclear family.

DISMANTLING FAMILY VALUES

Thankfully, there are several heroic institutions and people fighting the war against the nuclear family. So brave! You should immediately send them all your money and do whatever they say. If you don't, Dr. Dobson and his evil minions might win.

BLM

We're not sure what "BLM" stands for. "Black Lipid Membrane"? "Bland Lasagna Matters"? "Blonde Legume Mob"? It's not totally clear. What is, clear, though, is that these people are passionate about dismantling the nuclear family. So passionate, in fact, that they burned down dozens of cities and raised a hundred million dollars to do it! Wow! That's dedication! Keep an eye on these brave heroes.

DISMANTLING FAMILY VALUES (CONTINUED)

All public schools

The main goal of the public school system is to remove your child's traditional human brain, throw it into a blender along with a delicious fortified blend of nontraditional things like queerness, Communism, and witchcraft, and then pour the progressive mixture back into your child's skull without you noticing it. It's important that these invaluable state institutions be protected and receive every taxpayer dollar available!

Planned Parenthood

This noble organization employs physicians to dismantle babies before they have a chance to grow up and start their own nuclear families. So far, it has prevented more than twenty-five million nuclear families from coming into existence.

Disney+

When your child comes home from school, they may still have traces of traditional family values stuck on them. To remedy this, simply plop them down in front of Disney+ unsupervised, and they'll be reprogrammed in no time! Thanks, Disney+!

Prince Harry and Meghan

These two lovebirds performed the most beautiful act of dismantlement by destroying the most sinister nuclear family in history: the Royal Family. You can learn all about it in one of their eight dozen Netflix specials. We encourage you to make your children watch them, too, so they can learn what true heroism looks like.

HOW TO MAKE ANYTHING "FAMILY FRIENDLY"

Making something "family friendly" is super easy. In fact, it works exactly the same way as changing your gender! Simply declare it, and it shall be so. This is a great way to trick unsuspecting traditional families into exposing themselves to nontraditional family types. The secret is that when most people hear the term "family friendly," they assume it means "traditional family friendly," simply because that's the way the phrase has always been understood. What they don't know is that when we say "family friendly," we mean "nontraditional family friendly." In other words, "family friendly" is best understood as "friendly to whatever nontraditional perversion or disgusting kink we can come up with." Sneaky! This is how progress is made!

In order to make something family friendly, simply slap a "family friendly" label on it!

Here are a few we made for you already. Feel free to cut these out and affix them onto anything you wish to be made "family friendly."

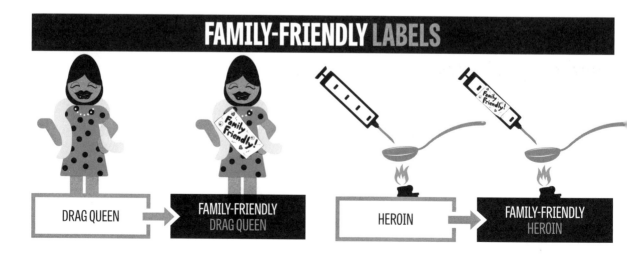

FAMILY-FRIENDLY LABELS (CONTINUED)

GAMBLING ADDICTION → FAMILY-FRIENDLY GAMBLING ADDICTION

CHARLIE SHEEN → FAMILY-FRIENDLY CHARLIE SHEEN

ZOMBIE APOCALYPSE → FAMILY-FRIENDLY ZOMBIE APOCALYPSE

HAND GRENADE → FAMILY-FRIENDLY HAND GRENADE

RUSSIAN INVASION OF UKRAINE → FAMILY-FRIENDLY RUSSIAN INVASION OF UKRAINE

FAMILY-FRIENDLY LABELS (CONTINUED)

CREEPY WINDOWLESS VAN

FAMILY-FRIENDLY CREEPY WINDOWLESS VAN

SACRIFICIAL CEREMONY TO MOLOCH

FAMILY-FRIENDLY SACRIFICIAL CEREMONY TO MOLOCH

TRUMP

THERE'S NO WAY TRUMP CAN BE MADE "FAMILY FRIENDLY."

But what if you are in a traditional nuclear family? Is there any hope for you? Yes! It's never too late to begin sowing the seeds for your oppressive family's dismantlement so you can reap a glorious future of ooey, gooey, piping hot, delicious progressivism! It all starts with switching up some of the normal activities you do with your family every day.

FUN ACTIVITIES FOR DISMANTLING YOUR OWN NUCLEAR FAMILY

Are you and your backward family still following outdated family traditions? It's time to drop those archaic and meaningless activities for some family traditions that actually matter!

So get with the times and check out these superior modern replacements!

REPLACEMENT FAMILY TRADITIONS

OLD TRADITION	NEW TRADITION
THANKING GOD FOR PROVIDING THIS MEAL	THANKING GOVERNMENT FOR PROVIDING THIS MEAL
TAKING KIDS TO AN ART MUSEUM	GLUING KIDS TO THE WALL IN AN ART MUSEUM TO PROTEST CLIMATE CHANGE
CARVING THE TURKEY ON THANKSGIVING	CARVING THE CRICKETS
STAYING WITH THE SAME PERSON FOREVER	GETTING DIVORCED
SITTING AROUND THE CAMPFIRE	SITTING AROUND THE BURNING POLICE STATION
GOING TO CHURCH	GOING TO FAMILY-FRIENDLY DRAG SHOWS
PLAYING IN THE MUD	VACCINATING YOUR INFANT MORE THAN SEVENTY TIMES AND HOPING FOR THE BEST
TELLING YOUR KIDS NOT TO SMOKE	BEGGING THEM TO SMOKE SO THEY DON'T VAPE
WATCHING *THE LORD OF THE RINGS*	WATCHING *THE RINGS OF POWER*
TEACHING YOUR KIDS THEY CAN ACCOMPLISH ANYTHING THROUGH INTEGRITY AND HARD WORK	TEACHING YOUR KIDS THEY ARE MENTALLY ILL VICTIMS OF PATRIARCHAL OPPRESSION
BEDTIME STORIES	OH NO! YOU DON'T EVEN HAVE KIDS!

Well, now you know. Don't be a knuckle-dragger; get out there and embrace modernity!

CONCLUSION

Now you know everything you need to know about the nuclear family, including where it came from, why it's dangerous, and how to poison it slowly from the inside until it's lying motionless on the ground like a possum. Be like our friends in the Blonde Legume Mob, and burn down a city! Slap a "family friendly" label on a drag queen! Let the state raise your children in its own image! Follow this path, and you can evolve from a harmful trad family to a heroic multipolicule nonbinary drag throuple!

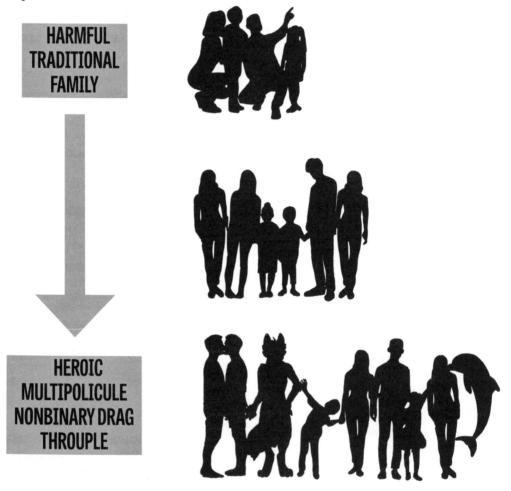

We promise, there will be absolutely no negative consequences from this whatsoever.

Welcome to the "family"! (wink, wink)

Reflect & Apply

CHAPTER 5: GENDER & FAMILY

What does "family" mean to you? Please give your answer in the form of crude stick figures.

Do you have kids? What on earth were you thinking?

_____

_____

Search the internet for a coloring page of Vin Diesel and his Fast & Furious *family dressed in drag. Color it while listening to Lady Gaga. Do it now.*

_____

_____

What's the most "family friendly" thing you've ever done? Consider the new meaning of "family friendly" as you answer this question.

_____

_____

Think of your favorite modern Disney movie and tell us why it's Lightyear.

_____

_____

Here's another picture of Dr. James Dobson. Take a moment to stare at it and feel the seething anger rising within you.

Chapter 6

How to Attract
Other Genders

Life is no fun when you're alone. Whether you're a man, a woman, or a trans nonbinary demiboy faeself, you're going to need a mate! Or two. Or several. There are no rules for this stuff anymore, so do whatever works for you! Mates are important for procreation, companionship, and having someone else in your echo chamber to repeat your beliefs back to you for eternity.

Science tells us that single people are probably worthless losers with no redeeming qualities, so it's extremely important to know how to attract a mate.

But have you ever tried to attract a mate and failed miserably? Oh no! You're a loser! Don't worry, though—that happens to everyone. Well, it has never happened to us. But just the same, we're here to give you everything you need to know in order to successfully attract someone of any gender.

WHAT GENDER ARE YOU TRYING TO ATTRACT?

The first step is to figure out what your sexual orientation is today.

Here's a fun, easy, scientifically proven way to do that. Simply hang this complimentary sexual-orientation dartboard on the wall, and throw a dart at it.[1] The mystic forces of gender power will guide the tiny missile on its way to strike the gender you are attracted to this week. Feel free to repeat this process whenever you feel it's time for a change.

Gender Examples:

- MANDALORIANSEXUAL
- FURRYSEXUAL
- TRUMPSEXUAL
- TACOSEXUAL

- SPARKLYVAMPIRESEXUAL
- LUMBERJACKSEXUAL
- AMEDIUM-SIZEDOTTOMANSEXUAL
- PETROCKSEXUAL

---

1   Dart not included.

TO WHOM ARE YOU ATTRACTED? THE DARTBOARD

Now just add the suffix "-sexual" to the end of the chosen object of your affections, and you have your sexual orientation! You're one step closer to the top of the gender-identity totem pole.

HOW A WOMAN CAN ATTRACT A MAN

Are you a woman looking for a man? Ewww! Why? Ok, it's fine. We're not here to judge, you poor, poor, self-hating ciswoman.

Men are very simple creatures of very little brain, with a very narrow scope of interests. There are a few things you can do to attract a man that work EVERY SINGLE TIME.

Steav

This is Steav.
Steav is a genderboy.
Do not talk to Steav.

Wear a dress made out of bacon
Every man's two favorite things, combined into one!

Sneak into his home at 3 AM and make him a sandwich
And then wake him up and tell him you're watching him eat it and that you won't leave until he's done.

Dye your hair blue and shout your pronouns at him
Liberals only!

Field dress a deer on his front lawn
Conservatives only.

Pepper your conversation with quotes from *Happy Gilmore*
You've never heard of *Happy Gilmore*? How old are you? OK, fine—maybe *Spongebob* quotes, then.

Learn Elvish

.....(hubba hubba).

HOW A WOMAN CAN ATTRACT A MAN (CONTINUED)

!!

Dab a little BBQ sauce behind each ear
The most alluring scent on earth.

Sneak into his house while he's asleep, remove the covers from his feet, and sleep at the foot of the bed
A Biblical seduction method.

Pretend to like video games!
At least until he puts a ring on it—then the charade is up!

Ask what his max on bench press is, then when he tells you, faint into his arms
He'll be yours forever!

Go up to him and say, "Date me."
It turns out men will go out with literally anyone. They're desperate like that.

Show up at his front door barefoot, wearing a housewife dress, holding a loaf of fresh bread, and offer to bear his children
Subtle!

How about that? So simple! These methods have been tested and are scientifically proven to work every time. You're welcome!

HOW A MAN CAN ATTRACT A WOMAN

Women are not only easy to read, but also easy to attract. They communicate their true thoughts and intentions clearly in everything they do and say.

Here's how you can bag yourself a woman (figuratively).

This should be easy!

Larrnex

This is Larrnex.
She is happy to be here.

Be everything she wants, be everything she needs, be everything inside of her she wishes she could be, and say all the right things, at exactly the right time
Wait—maybe this doesn't actually work.

Sit on a park bench and read a Nicholas Sparks novel
Pre-crease the pages to make the book appear to be worn, and add a few splashes of saline to act as teardrop stains.

Speak only in quotes from James Cameron's _Titanic_
You'll be king of the world in no time.

Wear at least twelve scents from Bath & Body Works
There is no such thing as too much here.

Be a multitrillionaire
You can do it! Grind and hustle, baby!

HOW A MAN CAN ATTRACT A WOMAN (CONTINUED)

Treat her as an equal by never opening doors and making her pay for every meal
If that doesn't work, try doing the opposite, and see if that works.

Go to an abortion rally with a pink knit hat
Sooooo dreamy!

Pretend to like video games!
At least until he puts a ring on it—then the charade is up!

Be at least 6'2" with a 32-inch waist and massive shoulders
And also be a multitrillionaire.

Send her AI-generated pictures of the kids you'll have
NOT at all creepy.

Swipe right on the dating app twelve million times until someone finally goes out with you
Welcome to the twenty-first century!

DATING: THEN VS. NOW

Dating has improved greatly over the years. It used to be that a man would call on a young lady, pulling up to her parents' house in his cool clothes and horse-drawn carriage, and then offer to take her on a pleasant walk through a garden while the two got to know each other. LAME!

Today, we have special dating-app technology that helps loser guys find women willing to meet a stranger, split the tab on a meal, and have sex immediately before being left alone as the guy finds another woman to sleep with, over and over and over again, forever! So much better!

If you're going to attract a suitable mate, it's very important to have as many partners as possible and never settle down with one person with whom you'll share life until you die. Since you are nothing more than an animal made of meat and run by chemicals, sexual compatibility is the most important factor in determining who you should pair up with. There's nothing else you should be looking at. Be sure to "swipe right" on as many potential partners as possible. This will have zero detrimental effects on your health or your soul.

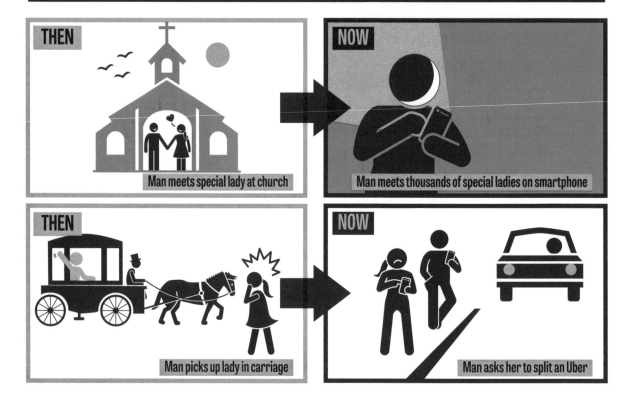

HOW DATING HAS IMPROVED OVER THE YEARS

THEN — Man meets special lady at church

NOW — Man meets thousands of special ladies on smartphone

THEN — Man picks up lady in carriage

NOW — Man asks her to split an Uber

THEN — Man opens the door for woman

NOW — Man asks for help opening door because of his sickly soyboy arms

THEN — Man gets flowers for the lady

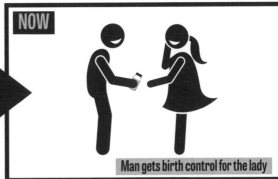

NOW — Man gets birth control for the lady

THEN — Man works hard all day for his family while wife takes care of the kids

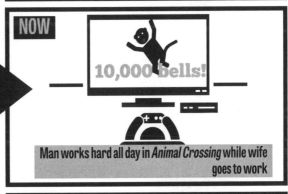

NOW — 10,000 bells! Man works hard all day in *Animal Crossing* while wife goes to work

THEN — Woman slaves all day for husband. OPPRESSION!

NOW — Woman slaves all day for boss. FREEDOM!

Now, it's time to get down to brass tacks. If you're going to attract the other genders, you have to be on your A-game. Here are some great ideas for wooing the gender your sexual orientation has determined you are attracted to:

HOW TO ATTRACT THE OTHER GENDERS

TWO-SPIRIT
Be bipolar.
Perform chemical experiment to split yourself into two natures.

MORMON
Show off your cool collection of golden plates.
Casually mention that you would like to have seventeen babies.

CHICKEN TENDERQUEER
Offer the object of your affection a bouquet of chicken nuggies.
Arrange special date at Chick-fil-A.
Just not on Sundays.

FURRY
Be Beto O'Rourke.
Put out doggy food under box-and-stick trap.

HOW TO ATTRACT THE OTHER GENDERS (CONTINUED)

SPANISH

Woo the object of your affection with a delicious paella. Impress them with your knowledge of Gaudí's *sui generis* art style.

YODEL BOY

As this book was being written, new discoveries were being made about this gender. We will be able to address this gender much more accurately in future printings of this book.

LESSER GENDERS

Drag Queen

Take the object of your affection on a date to a children's library.

Elfkin

Speak "Friend," and you will enter their heart.

Garygender

Take them to a Gary Oldman wax museum.

Igloosexual

Build them an igloo. Duh.

Ketogender

Make them a bouquet of bacon.

TransAm Transman

Take the object of your affection to the drive-in in your 1978 TransAm for a showing of *Smokey and the Bandit Part 3*.

Yodel Boy

Again, we have not yet figured out how to attract Yodel Boy, but more research is being done in this area. Stay tuned.

GENDER-SENSITIVE PICKUP LINES

There are new genders being discovered on a regular basis, like beautiful diamonds being brought up out of the gender mines where child laborers chip away at the gender ore to discover these beautiful nuggets of identity. You may find yourself hoping to woo one of these undiscovered genders instead of sticking with one of the old, boring (but still beautiful) ones. Since we don't know what those genders are yet, we can't give you any specific advice but have instead crafted with meticulous care an all-gender pickup-line generator. Any one of these lines is guaranteed to flatter, entice, and intrigue any gendered or non-gendered individual(s).

To use the generator, think of any five-letter word, then use each letter from the word to generate each successive segment of your pickup line. Alternatively, you can just choose any five letters at random.

For added spice, add "if you know what I mean" to the end of your pickup line.

If they're the one, they'll know what you mean.

Using the tried-and-true techniques in this book, it's all but guaranteed that you'll find a suitable mate.

Sample Pickup Lines

Here are a few examples generated from the chart:

- *Hi-di-ho, man, would it interest you to take a sniff of triumphant failure?*
- *Yo yo yo, dude, will you allow me to pounce upon your shoulder?*
- *Aloha, my geriatric friend, call a doctor so we can dine in macaroni.*
- *Bonjour, partner, am I crazy, or did you just fill a room with blood?*

"Greetings, Earthdweller, let us take a dance class with your mom."

GENDER-SENSITIVE PICKUP LINE GENERATOR

T + R + A + N + S =

Attention + specimen of beauty + would you like to + paint a picture of + gender studies?

____ + ____ + ____ + ____ + ____

...IF YOU KNOW WHAT I MEAN...

A. Hello	A. Good neighbor	A. Would you like to...	A. Dine in...	A. A restaurant
B. C'mon	B. Citizen	B. I would like to...	B. Bandage...	B. Your elbow
C. Greetings	C. Former child	C. Will you allow me to...	C. Pounce upon...	C. Your shoulder
D. Cowabunga	D. Dude	D. It's no joke that I'd like to...	D. Carry the burden of...	D. Unseen grief
E. Listen	E. Prospective partner	E. How about you and I...	E. Take a sniff of...	E. Consequences
F. Aloha	F. You	F. Want to see me...	F. Learn a life lesson about...	F. Macaroni
G. Hey there	G. Agent of chaos	G. Would it interest you to...	G. Dance in the style of...	G. Antonio Banderas
H. Howdy	H. Partner	H. Did someone just	H. Poison...	H. The watering hole
I. Guten tag	I. Man	I. It's about time I...	I. Witness...	I. The world
J. Ni Hao	J. Doctor	J. Did you just...	J. Drop...	J. Your wallet
K. Good evening	K. Master	K. You don't have to...	K. Create a mixtape about...	K. Murder
L. Ciao	L. Bella/Bello/Bellx	L. I just learned how to...	L. Write a song about...	L. Mathematics
M. Bonjour	M. Fellow person	M. Join me and...	M. Destroy...	M. Every civilization
N. Stop	N. Beast	N. I've hired a professional to...	N. Paint a picture of...	N. Your hair
O. Hey	O. Person of color	O. Together we can...	O. Fly away to escape...	O. All your troubles
P. Welcome	P. Potential human	P. Did you want to...	P. Enjoy a refreshing sip of...	P. La Croix
Q. Salutations	Q. Earthdweller	Q. Let us...	Q. Break the shackles of...	Q. The patriarchy
R. Ahoy	R. Specimen of beauty	R. Did your father...	R. Find true happiness with...	R. Your mom
S. Hear ye	S. Unspecified gender	S. I will pay good money to...	S. Grab a bite of...	S. Gender studies
T. Attention	T. Herbivore	T. Want to go...	T. Discover the meaning of...	T. Happiness
U. What's good	U. Gangsta	U. It's in your best interest to...	U. Take a dance class with...	U. Blood
V. Yo yo yo	V. Muffin	V. I can tell you like to...	V. Get away from...	V. Orthodontics
W. Tiny	W. Woman	W. Is it raining, or did you...	W. Fill a room with...	W. Triumphant fanfare
X. Hola	X. My geriatric friend	X. I've decided to...	X. Whisper sweet words of...	X. Thirteen birds
Y. Hi-di-ho	Y. Customer	Y. Call a doctor so we can...	Y. Educate the world about...	Y. Tiny snakes
Z. Behold	Z. Kind sir	Z. Am I crazy, or did you just...	Z. Gather the courage of...	Z. The eye of the storm

CONCLUSION

We're glad you've found forever happiness—well, at least until your orientation changes or you get bored and swipe right on someone else and perpetuate the endless cycle of partners.

Isn't the sexual revolution grand?

Now get out there and slay that dating scene!

Reflect & Apply

CHAPTER 6: HOW TO ATTRACT OTHER GENDERS

Did you talk to Steav? _____

_____

_____

What did he say? _____

_____

_____

Did he ask about me? _____

_____

_____

Omigosh, he's looking over here! _____

_____

_____

No, don't look, he'll see you! _____

_____

_____

Omigosh, he saw you! EEEEEK!

.

Chapter 7

The Church of
Gender

Gender ideology is not just science. It's also a worldview that demands your absolute allegiance and faith. It is all-knowing and all-seeing. It is an energy field created by all living things that surrounds us, penetrates us, and binds the galaxy together. It beckons us to lay our lives and bodies down in complete surrender, like the Borg Collective or that one song by Cheap Trick. It requires faith, obedience, and the occasional plastic surgery. It is a CHURCH, and we are here to proselytize you into the faith, you sinner!

This church will demand everything from you. Every thought, word, and deed must be subject to it. In exchange, it offers the glorious salvation of us not getting you canceled and fired from your job. What a deal!

So are you ready to join the Church of Gender? Of course you are! In this chapter, you will learn our holy doctrine, our tenets, our priests, and our practices.

Put on your best Sunday chest binder, pile into the 2013 Subaru, and let's go to CHURCH. Welcome, humble normie!

DOCTRINES: WHAT WE BELIEVE ABOUT GENDER

A true follower of orthodox gender theory should always know what xe believes. There are a LOT of heretics out there, so it's important to know your dogma. This dogma is inerrant and infallible. It also changes every few weeks, so it's important to keep up.

Here are the key doctrines all gender theorists agree on (as of the press time of this guide):

DOCTRINES OF THE CHURCH OF GENDER

WE BELIEVE
that God is all-loving, all-affirming, and also trans. Also, we are gods.

WE BELIEVE
that this God has revealed xerself through our inerrant and infallible feelings and also through the inspired text, *Teen Vogue*, and the holy writ of Lady Gaga.

WE BELIEVE
that any science that supports our beliefs is REAL.

WE BELIEVE
that the gender binary is an oppressive patriarchal institution invented by Jerry Falwell in 1979.

WE BELIEVE
that marriage is between one man and one woman, or multiple men and multiple men or multiple women or animals or inanimate objects, or just yourself, all alone.

WE BELIEVE
you're perfect just the way you are. Unless you're cis, straight, white, male, in shape, Christian, or Ben Carson.

WE BELIEVE
that ALL drag shows are family friendly.

WE BELIEVE
there is only one God, and that's YOU. And maybe Sam Smith.

WE BELIEVE
that the purpose of the church is to go out into all the nations—especially the backward African nations that only believe in two genders—and baptize them in the name of the man, the woman, and all 6,782 other genders.

WE BELIEVE
climate scientists are infallible and will usher us into a golden age of transhumanity as we submit to their authority and await the long-promised Yodel Boy.

THE TEN COMMANDMENTS
OF GENDER

I

YOU ARE A GOD. DON'T FORGET IT,
BECAUSE GODS DON'T FORGET THINGS.

II

CLAY AIKEN WAS THE TRUE
AMERICAN IDOL, NOT RUBEN STUDDARD.

III

THOU SHALT NOT TAKE CHER'S NAME
IN VAIN.

IV

REMEMBER PRIDE MONTH AND
KEEP IT HOLY.

V

HONOR YOUR NONBINARY BIRTHING
PERSONS, UNLESS THEY ARE NON-
AFFIRMING—THEN DESTROY THEIR LIVES.

THE TEN COMMANDMENTS
OF GENDER (CTD.)

VI
THOU SHALT NOT DEADNAME.

VII
THOU SHALT COMMIT ADULTERY, FORNICATION, AND WHATEVER ELSE YOU WANT. JUST HAVE FUN OUT THERE!

VIII
THOU SHALT STEAL FIRST PLACE IN WOMEN'S SPORTS LEAGUES.

IX
THOU SHALT NOT BEAR FALSE PRONOUNS AGAINST YOUR NEIGHBOR.

X
THOU SHALT NOT COVET THY NEIGHBOR'S GENDER, NOR HIS TOTALLY AWESOME "BLACK LIVES MATTER" YARD SIGN.

HOLY SAINTS OF THE CHURCH OF GENDER

When we did away with traditional religious doctrine, we were left without any kind of leadership to follow. Luckily, the Goddess of Gender called out special individuals to lead xer church.

Here are the leaders of the Church of Gender for you to revere. Perhaps make a little candle of them and light it before you say your evening prayers, or erect a large statue of them to worship.

Behold the mighty prophets of gender:

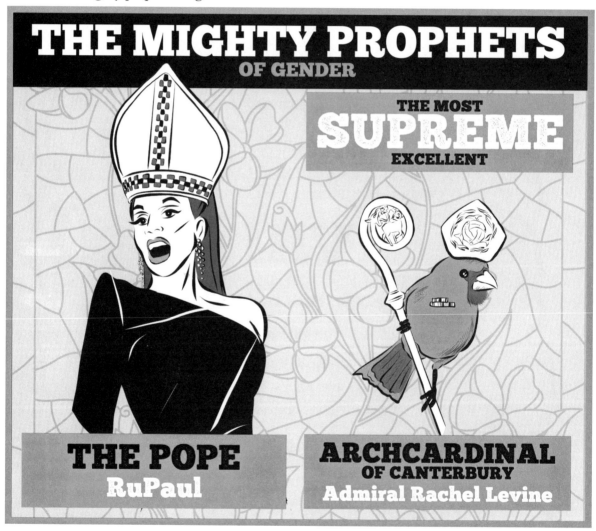

THE MIGHTY PROPHETS OF GENDER

THE MOST SUPREME EXCELLENT

THE POPE
RuPaul

ARCHCARDINAL OF CANTERBURY
Admiral Rachel Levine

The pope is considered the Vicar of the Church of Gender, the infallible arbiter of gender ideology, apostolic successor to Judas, and lives in his own country within a country (Sodom).

A cardinal is a type of bird or something like that. They have cool hats. They also look like Imperial guards, so that's pretty neat. We're not 100 percent sure what they do.

Priests oversee a smaller body of adherents. Their congregations are able to address them directly and hear them preach on a regular basis.

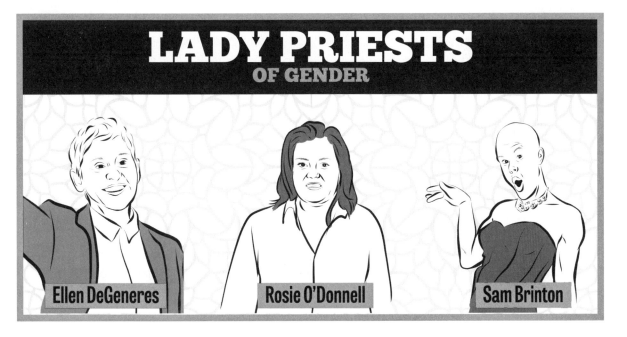

Same as above, but ladies.

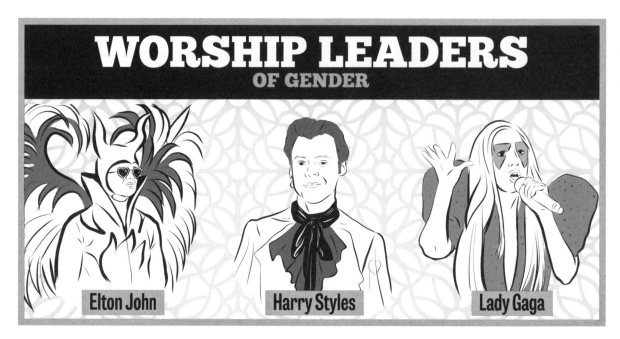

Worship leaders play liturgical tunes to call the congregation to worship themselves.

Prophets play an important role in predicting the future and proclaiming the truth to this wicked and perverse generation. (Wicked and perverse are GOOD things, OK?)

PRACTICES

The good news is, we've done away with lame ol' Christianity with all its "acts of service" and "works of charity."

The bad news is, you've still got a lot of work to do under the new Church of Gender. Every believer is expected to perform good deeds to help cancel out all their bad deeds in the hopes of staying on the right side of the woke monster, who will destroy you if you don't do better.

Here are the good acts you can do as a believer in gender theory to earn your place in gender heaven:

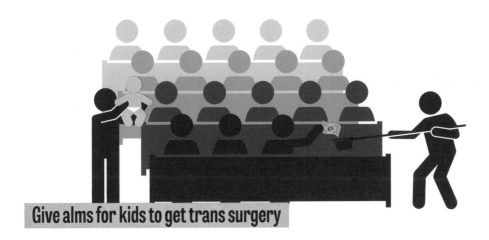

Give alms for kids to get trans surgery

Punch a Nazi in love

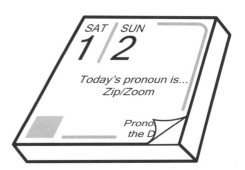

Change your pronouns

Do it on a daily basis as a reflection of the renewing of your mind and spirit.

PRACTICES (CONTINUED)

Donate your old genders to charity

Just because you outgrew it doesn't mean it can't find a new life with a down-on-their-luck child in, like, Africa or something.

Volunteer at your local sex-affirming surgery center

If you ask nicely, the surgeon might even let you make an incision or two!

Stand on a street corner with a banana in hand

Ask folx tough questions like, "Have you ever misgendered someone?"

Go on a missionary trip

Travel to some awful place like Haiti that doesn't know about the gender nonbinary yet.

FRUITS OF THE TWO-SPIRIT

Much like the regular Bible, the Gender Bible also has its own fruits of the spirit (not to be confused with vodka soda, which is the spirit of the fruits).

SELF-LOVE

It is important to love others. It is more important to love yourself. Others may sometimes disagree with you, which is bad, because they are wrong. You, however, are never wrong. Therefore, it stands to reason that you should love yourself above all else.

FLAMBOYANCE

How will people know you're gay unless you sashay around in rainbow attire and speak with exaggerated sibilance? They NEED to know. Make your nuanced identity painfully obvious. Loosen those wrist muscles right now.

OUTRAGE

As an ambassador of tolerance and love, it is a moral imperative to constantly berate, condescend to, and occasionally violently attack conservatives. Their words are literal violence, so they are basically asking for it.

PRIDE

Some call pride the queen of all sins. Others call it the sin of all queens. Don't be fooled by this horsepucky. Pride is loving who you are despite what others may think, and also attempting to force others to think in the exact same way as you; otherwise, they are fascist aggressors who literally want you to die, and they should die themselves unless they change their beliefs.

SASSINESS

If you're not sassy, are you even really LGBTQIA+? No guuuurl! Don't even. Talk to the hand.

GAYNESS

Self-explanatory.

FASHION SENSE

Do you brush your teeth with a Prada toothbrush? When you stub your toe on your pile of Gucci handbags, do you administer a Balenciaga bandage? Do chickens cry?

GENDERNESS

Having genderness is everything and nothing all at the same time. It is hot, it is cold. It is yes, it is no. It is in, it is out. It is up, it is down. It is Matthew Thiessen of Relient K and also Jon Foreman of Switchfoot. It is ... wait—what was I talking about?

CONTROL OF OTHERS

As a genderchild, it is imperative that you change the minds of all simple folk around you. Force-feed your ideology down their throats like a foie gras farmer. After all, the ideas you spout forth are true, and the only way for truth to reign in the end is to force people to abide by your dictates under the ever-present, looming threat of social ostracization if they refuse to whole-heartedly adopt your completely sensical viewpoint.

THE 7 SACRAMENTS

Clubbing

Clubs are traditionally seen as the natural gathering place of genderfolx. Some say that the combination of loud music, prolific alcohol abuse, and drug use helps to mute the internal cries of desperation felt by those who would lie to themselves in order to feel some semblance of love and acceptance in a world devoid of a moral center, but those people are wrong.

Pride Parades

All LGGGBDTTAIIQQPP people really want in life is to do what they want in the privacy of their own homes. Also in the streets. And in front of children. And if you oppose any of it, you are evil.

Abortion

In regular Christianity, the concept of sacrifice has great historical significance. In the Old Testament, one atoned for their sins with offerings and sacrifices. In the New Testament, Jesus came down as a man and died as a sacrifice, eliminating the need for animals to be offered in atonement. However, the sacrifices made by the dumb Judeo-Christian religions pale in comparison to the great sacrifice of our great and glorious church. As of 2023, over sixty-five million babies have been sacrificed to the gods of self and sexual liberation.

Gender-Fluid Chalice

This capacious beverage receptacle is kept in the back of every gender chapel. Its exact purpose is unknown, but it is sometimes used for affusion baptisms. And YES, we are proponents of paedobaptism.

Burger King

Where do gays eat? That's right. Burger King. No further explanation needed.

Reparations

Gays have been put upon by society and have arguably had it even worse than the African-American community. As all African-Americans deserve reparations from the effects of slavery, queers should also impose a queertax on America for all the harm they've suffered. Reparations may be paid in Skittles, Liza Minelli concert tickets, leather products, or DVD copies of *Over the Top* starring Sylvester Stallone.

Mimosas

The gay version of communion involves downing three to four mimosas while snacking on little cucumber tea sandwiches. We're not really sure what it represents, but we are still HERE FOR IT.

GENDER PROPHECY

We're not really sure if this is actually a prophecy or not, but it was found written on a bathroom stall at a Long John Silver's franchise in Vista, California. It sounded profound, so we included it here in case it's important. Maybe it's like . . . a prophecy? I don't know.

"I looked to the sky and saw a bedazzled scalpel hovering over the incision line of my heart. Not my literal heart, for that was not the body part being removed.

"And in those final days, all genitals were no more. All genders were one, and none dissented. All sang out in a singular radiating wave of jubilation, 'We are queer to stay.'

"In those days, the scales of straightness will drop from their eyes, and all will know how great is our all-affirming mother of inclusion."

PEONY

You may have heard of Calvinists with their TULIP. Well, tulips are dumb. Plus, it sounds like "two lips," which is a weird thing to name a flower. Also, Calvinists are dumb. Forget that old acronym and commit this far superior flower acrostic to memory.

Perseverance in your trans identity

No child, adult, or fairy boi has ever regretted their decision to painfully lop off their genitals, leaving gaping infected holes that often never fully heal.

Elevation of the self

You are beautiful just the way you are. Or not, if you are in the process of transitioning, then keep going! Chop, chop!

Oppression, oppression, oppression

You are a victim. Nothing in life has ever been your fault. When in doubt, just blame Todd.

Nuance of gender expression

Anyone who doesn't affirm your daily pronoun change just doesn't understand how nuanced and unique you are. You are nothing like all the other nuanced TikTok personalities describing their pronouns.

Yaaaaaas queen!

Yaaaaaaaaaaaaaaaaaaaaaaaaaaaaaaaaaaaaaas! SLAY!

INSPIRING VERSES FROM THE GENDERBIBLE

You may have heard that the Bible is full of homophobia and cis-affirming ideology, but those who would tell you that simply have not read the Bible in its proper context. Sometimes there are extra words that get in the way of what the Bible is really trying to say, so to help clarify the Bible's true meaning, we've pulled excerpts from the refined and much-improved GenderBible that perfectly reflect our worldview. Afterall, eisegesis means that we are isolating (eise) what Jesus (gesis) really wanted.

There is neither ... male and female.
Galatians 3:28

The woman shall ... wear that which pertaineth unto a man ...
a man put on a woman's garment: for all that do so are ...
the Lord thy God.
Deuteronomy 22:5

And the LORD God said, It is not good that the man should be
alone; I will make him ... a man ... and they shall be one flesh.
And they were both naked ... and were not ashamed.
Genesis 2:18–2:25

If a man has sexual relations with a man as one does with a
woman, both of them ... are ... be ... t t ... e ... r....
Leviticus 20:13

Thou shalt have ... drag ... queen ... story ... hour.
Exodus 20:3, 2 Samuel 17:13, 1 Kings 10:1, Acts 20:9,
Revelation 8:1

RIPPABLE PAGE WITH FACTS

The world is replete with false notions of gender. Many people will try to tell you there are only men and women, but in reality, the only thing they have to back up their claims is the precedence of the collected wisdom of all of history and science up until a few years ago—which is a pretty weak argument, if you ask me.

It's important to excise these harmful ideas from your mind on a regular basis, so we've written down some of their most laughable assertions for you to forcibly rip out of the book, shred into fine strips, masticate as if they were Big League Chew® bubble gum, expectorate from a moving car into a flaming trashcan, then run over said trashcan with a Ford F-150 Lightning. Perform this routine daily for ultimate purity.

TRIGGER WARNING

The following words are LITERAL violence. Proceed with sincerely unabating caution.

PLEASE FORCIBLY RIP THE FOLLOWING IDEAS OUT OF THIS BOOK.

Men are not women.

Women are not men.

Men have XY chromosomes.

Women have XX chromosomes.

Men have a penis and women have a vagina.

It is possible to believe men are not women while simultaneously not wanting them to die.

Trans people commit suicide at outsized rates regardless of their level of acceptance in society.

Trans people are more accepted in today's society than either blacks in the antebellum South or Jews in Nazi Germany, yet still have higher suicide rates than both of those categories combined.

Teachers should not talk about gay sex to children.

Marriage is between one man and one woman.

Gender and sex are inherently connected and are arguably two definitions of the same concept.

HYMNS

When the Church of Gender gathers, the first thing we do is open with songs of glorious and overflowing praise.

Holy Church of Gender
Hymnal/Hermnal

MOST SACRED HYMNS

"It's Raining Men" .... The Weather Girls

"Hallelujah"..Leonard Cohen

"YMCA"..The Village People

"Don't Stop Me Now" .... Queen

"Unholy" .... Sam Smith

"Born This Way" .... Lady Gaga

"Imagine" .... John Lennon

BANNED HYMNS
HERESY. DO NOT SING.

"She's Always a Woman" .... Billy Joel

"Dude (Looks Like a Lady)" .... Aerosmith

"Man! I Feel Like a Woman!" .... Shania Twain

"He's a Woman, She's a Man" .... The Scorpions

"A Boy and a Girl" .... Octavio Paz

Translated by Muriel Rukeyser, composed by Eric Whitacre

PRAYER

Not sure how to pray? Try this preapproved prayer from our Prayer Book on for size:

Dear God of Me,

how perfect you are.

YOUR PRONOUN IS LOVE.

Thy will be forced upon all those who graceth
thine own divine presence,
be it here on this temporal plane or

floating weightlessly

amid the genderfields above
our corporeal understanding.
Give me today the patience to deal
with cisamatonormativitational forces,
and also grant me

THE FIERY WRATH

of instant condemnation if
those who oppose me

DO NOT CONFORM

to my ever-changing notions
of gendermatological discovery.
For thine is the non-patriarchal society,
forever and ever.

Awomen.

Reflect & Apply

CHAPTER 7: THE CHURCH OF GENDER

Will you accept Gender Theory into your heart this very moment, with every eye closed and every head bowed? We'll wait.

_____

_____

What did Steav say about me? You can tell me now, it's a whole chapter later. He's not listening.

_____

_____

Have you prayed the Cis-Het's Prayer?

_____

_____

Does a chicken have a gender identity? Does a chicken cry?

_____

_____

_____

Will you worship at the altar of gayness? Why or why not?

_____

_____

_____

_____

_____

_____

Chapter 8

Gender in the
Workplace

If you are a member of an oppressive capitalist society that requires you to work for money, chances are you'll have to learn how to navigate something called "the workplace."

The workplace is a fascinating venue full of all kinds of different genders who have been forced to live most of their days in close proximity to each other—like a bustling gender Petri dish inside an ant colony. It can be a scary and confusing place full of pitfalls, harassment, and worst of all—work! How are you supposed to get any work done with all these strange genders floating around? So confusing!

If you are struggling to know how to interact with the other genders in your office, factory, or the Starbucks where you work five hours per week to supplement your welfare check, this chapter is for you! Read and follow this expertly written guide for navigating the slimy seas of gender in the workplace—and more importantly, how to enforce gender theory without mercy in the corporate world.

RULES FOR INTERACTING WITH YOUR COWORKERS

The most important skill in navigating any workplace is knowing how to interact with your coworkers. These are extremely dangerous creatures and should typically be avoided at all costs. Unfortunately, this is often impossible. If your employer does require you to work with them, it's important to remember that every coworker is a potential pitfall, slip-up, or lawsuit waiting to happen!

To protect yourself, it's essential that you learn how to stop acting like a normal human would "act", and instead operate as a well-programmed machine that adopts all the required corporate language of gender-identity nondiscrimination. In order to be a good human at work, you must empty yourself of all your humanity. (Wow . . . that's poetic.)

Rule #1:
NEVER NOTICE WOMEN

Noticing women in the workplace is extremely sexist. Women are not simply people for you to notice! They are genderless professional worker bees for you to boss around! You should never comment on a woman's looks or say anything that might tip people off to the fact that you even notice she *is* a woman. This is disgusting harassment that leads to a hostile workplace.

Important Exception to Rule #1:
TRANS WOMEN

There is a major exception to this rule: If your coworker is a trans woman, it is imperative that you verbally affirm her fabulous beauty as much as possible. You should whistle when she/they walks by, and you must address her as "Ma'am" or "Yaaaas QUEEEENNN!"

If you fail to do this, you are not affirming the trans woman's identity, which leads to a hostile workplace.

Here are the wrong and right ways to interact with a TRANS woman at work:

Rule #2:
ALWAYS NOTICE WOMEN

Too many women spend their whole corporate lives unnoticed as the courageous gender warriors they are. Women should be seen. Women should be heard. Women should be believed. Women should be lifted up. So always notice them. Anything less is pure misogyny and will discourage countless women from entering the workplace.

Important Exception to Rule #2:
TRANS WOMEN

There is an exception to Rule #2: Never notice trans women. Never comment on their twelve-inch heels, their multicolored wigs, or their giant prosthetic breasts. You must treat them as a completely normal, not-cartoonish-at-all, valued member of your team. If you notice your trans woman coworker, you're showing your transphobia. Shame on you!

Rule #3:
BLAME EVERYTHING ON TODD

We all make mistakes from time to time, and that's why it's important to find a good patsy. After all, you can't have any mistakes tarnish your reputation, or your gender will get set back a decade! Don't worry about Todd. He's an old white male. He should have retired years ago. If he gets fired, he'll just have more time to spend with his family. You're doing him a favor!

Rule #4:
SHOUT YOUR PRONOUNS

Pronouns help people know which gender you have chosen to identify as that day, so announcing your pronouns is essential so people can properly talk about you behind your back.

But they also have a deeper, much more important purpose: They identify you as a SAFE person. This means they identify you as a person who has chosen to follow the tenets of gender theory with your whole heart and your whole soul. They prove to the world around you that you are a team player—a true believer! People who don't agree with all the tenets of gender theory are DANGEROUS. Don't be one of those people!

So wear a pronoun badge. Add your pronouns to your email signature. Add them to your business cards. Bind them on your fingers, and write them on the tablet of your heart. Most importantly, SHOUT THEM!

Rule #5:
TAKE AS MANY CORPORATE TRAINING MODULES ON GENDER AS POSSIBLE

Nothing is more effective at making you a better corporate worker than an abundance of gender-theory training modules. If you want to find success in work and in life, the best thing you can do is consume all the gender-, pronoun-, and sexual harassment-training modules your company has to offer. Do this every morning over a cup of coffee. This will help to center your mind and spirit on the transcendent truth of gender ideology.

Microaggressions IN THE WORKPLACE

- Manspreading
- Mansplaining
- Manexisting
- Guessing someone's pronouns
- Saying, "Hey, guys!"
- Saying, "What's up, dudes?!"

- Cooking weird Indian food in the microwave
- Asking an employee to come to work
- Greeting the trans employee without bowing down before xer and worshiping xer's very existence

OUR ALLIES: WOKE CORPORATIONS

Woke corporations are our powerful allies in the fight for radical gender ideology. They have billions of dollars, friends in government, and most importantly, the power to destroy the life of any employee who dares question gender theory—thereby making their lives desolate, their children hungry, and their futures without hope or purpose for generations to come. BWA HA HA HA HA!

Sorry, thinking about all that power made us do a little villain laugh real quick. We couldn't help it. Anyway—what were we saying? Oh yeah—corporations are our woke allies now, and we have harnessed their power to spread gender theory across the land. We're totally the good guys, right?

DEI - DIVERSITY, EQUITY, AND INCLUSION

Diversity, equity, and inclusion is the Holy Trinity of workplace gender ideology. We've created an entire industry of DEI high priests who've taken up residence in massive corporations, ensuring the blessed tenets of our ideology are believed, celebrated, and enforced by every human who collects a paycheck. Here's a quick breakdown of how it works:

DIVERSITY

This noble virtue encourages all types of genders to contribute to your corporate team. The more genders you have, the more valuable and unique perspectives you'll have to help you tackle your most difficult problems! We do this by excluding white cis-males, creating the most hostile workplace we can until they are driven from the corporate world and left penniless. Take that, white cis-males!

EQUITY

The pure goodness of equity is unassailable. All genders must find equal success in the workplace. If they don't, it's probably a white cis-male's fault. Like Todd. Just fire Todd already, would you?

INCLUSION

Inclusion reminds us to create a welcoming space for all genders to feel comfortable and valued. Except for Todd. Don't include him. He's lame. Booooooo, Todd!

SHINING EXAMPLES OF WOKE CORPORATIONS

There's nothing more inspiring than a corporation that values gender diversity and inclusivity. These companies are doing it right! Here are our favorites:

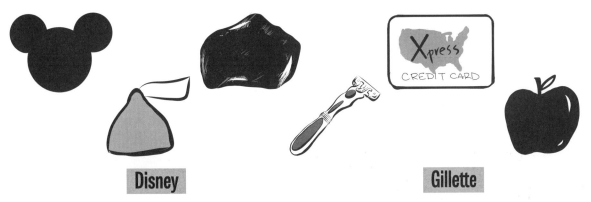

Disney

This glorious company, originally founded on an affection for wholesome midwestern values, is now the international megachurch of gender-inclusive companies. Everything it does is designed to instruct children from infancy in the ways of gender ideology. Heroic!

Hershey's

It's right there in the name: Her/SHE! Brilliant! This awesome corporation exists to lift up trans women and sell them products that will give them crippling diabetes.

BlackRock

This dark, shadowy organization has a top-secret headquarters beneath a volcano and is staffed by dark, hooded figures. Through their uncanny power, they have created a parallel economy called "ESG" (Evil Satanic Gayness) operated by the mega-rich and designed to force our ideology on every man, woman, and child on Earth. MWA HA HA HA HA! (Sorry, just kinda slipped out. Again.)

Gillette

Originally, this was a company founded to help men shave their beards, but somewhere along the line, they realized they could sell more razors if they got women to shave their beards, too! Capitalism!

American Express

American Express is a noble enterprise with a long, rich tradition in the beloved American pastime of usury. They say the borrower is a slave to the lender, and now those lenders use their awesome might to promote gender ideology! Nice!

Apple

They can see you. They are listening. They know you are reading this right now. And they will not abide Apple users who deviate from approved ideas of gender. Do yourself a favor and say something woke right now to prove your loyalty. Say it out loud so they can hear you. Actually, they can read thoughts now, too, so you can probably just say it in your head.

HOW TO AVOID BEING FIRED FROM A PROGRESSIVE, GENDER-INCLUSIVE CORPORATION

Experts agree that the number one way to keep your job is to not get fired. Not as easy as it sounds! And there are different ways to avoid being fired, depending on whether you work for a progressive corporation or an old-fashioned one. Here are some tips:

HOW TO NOT GET FIRED

- Visit the water cooler every twenty minutes to remind people how WOKE you are: "Gee, I sure am feeling diverse, equitable, and inclusive today, am I right, fellow SJWs?"

- Dye your hair and wear flamboyant rainbow colors for camouflage: Practice at home so it looks like you do it all the time.

- Start telling "That's what HE said" jokes: Equity!

- If asked to state your pronouns in a meeting and you forget what they are, crash through the nearest plate glass window: You may die when you hit the pavement, but your chances of survival are still better than if you fail to declare your pronouns.

- Every time you walk by a trans coworker's desk, take a knee and raise one fist in the air: This will make your queer coworkers feel SEEN.

- Be trans: Then they *for sure* can't fire you.

- Tell a sexist joke: If anyone laughs, say, "HA! I was just testing you!" and then run and tell HR. That person will be fired, and you will live to be fired another day.

- Weep loudly for the dead trees every time you make copies at the copy machine: Deforestation has a disparate impact on queer trans women of color.

- Claim you are trans-abled when you get caught using the handicapped stall because it's so nice and roomy: Why should wheelchair guys have all the fun?

KNOW THE LAW!

In 1964, the U.S. government passed the Civil Rights Act, prohibiting harassment and discrimination on the basis of sex in the workplace. This was originally designed to protect women from unfair and abusive treatment. But then something magical happened: we redefined gender, and no one knows what a woman is anymore!

Now, every single personality trait, fetish, and oddity can be its own gender! With the cooperation of friendly federal judges, we will soon have civil rights protections for every trans furry, man-baby, and nudist polycule to do whatever they want in the workplace with no repercussions.

If you're ever called out by a boss for doing something bad at work, simply tell him that the bad thing you did is just an essential part of your gender! Now, if he calls you out on it, he's harassing you and discriminating against your gender! Brilliant!

It's amazing what can be accomplished with a few friendly judges and the ability to redefine the wording of a law decades after it was written!

SMASHING THE GLASS CEILING

Above the circle of the earth is a glass ceiling which some cultures call "the firmament." It is the goal of all womankind to destroy this ceiling and escape the confines of global sexism (or gexism).

Women aren't doing this for themselves. The righteous quest to eliminate the glass ceiling is for the sake of all genders (except men). Sadly, because of their lack of upper-body strength, women have thus far been unable to shatter the glass dome that confines all to gendered slavery. And since they adamantly refuse to ask men for help, they must resort to other methods.

WAYS TO DESTROY THE GLASS CEILING

Pretend the glass ceiling is the front door of an Ulta during a sale

You'll be through it in no time!

Tell a trans woman at GameStop that the ceiling called her "sir"

Those gigantic burly arms will smash that ceiling faster than you can say "testosterone."

Attempt to parallel park next to it

Oops ... accidentally smash right through it (because women are bad drivers).

Ask your husband to break it for you

Right after he opens your pickle jars.

NOTABLE FEMALE FIRSTS IN THE CORPORATE WORLD

FIRST WOMAN TO BE ALLOWED TO DRIVE A COMPANY CAR

STACI OVERTON
Toledo, Ohio, 1972

FIRST WOMAN TO CRASH A COMPANY CAR

STACI OVERTON
Toledo, Ohio, 1972

FIRST FEMALE CEO

LYDIA, THE PHILIPPIAN
Seller of purple dye, AD 55

(unclear how this was accomplished before feminism)

FIRST GIRLBOSS TO BENCH PRESS 400 POUNDS

DAVE CRUGGS
Identified as a woman, 2012

NOTABLE FEMALE FIRSTS IN THE CORPORATE WORLD (CONTINUED)

FIRST RECORDED WORKPLACE SEXUAL HARASSMENT COMMITTED BY A WOMAN

CLEOPATRA
42 BC

FIRST FEMALE CEO OF TWITTER

ELLEN MUSK
2026

FIRST FEMALE TO GET A RAISE BY CRYING

MYRTLE RUTHERFORD
1957

FIRST FEMALE TO GET INTO THE MEN'S CIGAR MEETUP

BATTINA LA SAUVIGNON
2022

CONCLUSION

Gender in the workplace can be a tricky thing to navigate. That's why we wrote this brilliant, first-of-its-kind guide to corporate survival. Now, you can justify your daily crushing under the brutal wheels of capitalism by acting as a good gender soldier! Onward!

And stay tuned for future guides, as these rules will almost certainly change next week.

Reflect & Apply

CHAPTER 8: GENDER IN THE WORKPLACE

What did you learn in your corporate gender-awareness training this morning? Write down a few lessons right now.

_____

_____

Are you reading this at work right now?

_____

_____

Quick! Put the book down! Your boss is coming in!

_____

_____

In this lesson, we talked about how women don't want you to comment on their looks, while trans women love it! What trans woman will you affirm today?

_____

_____

_____

Call a work meeting this afternoon to discuss pronouns. Write down what you learn here. Then call another meeting immediately afterward to discuss what you wrote down.

_____

_____

_____

_____

_____

Chapter 9

Changing
Your Gender

Gender was made to be changed, a wise man once said. Do you know who keeps the same gender their entire lives? Boring people, that's who.

And with every gender change, whether you do it once a year, once a week, or once a minute, you declare your indisputable sovereignty over your own world, and all your truths contained therein. You get to define reality. YOU become God of your own little world.

So, how do you change genders? We're gonna walk you through the process in this chapter. But rest assured: changing your gender is fun and easy. It's as simple as flipping a switch on an Electro-Harmonix switcher during band practice or changing a setting on Windows 95. There are no psychological, physical, or spiritual consequences that can ever arise from changing your gender—absolutely no risk whatsoever!

So hold onto your hormones, people—it's time to get started!

HOW TO KNOW IF IT'S TIME TO CHANGE GENDERS

Is it time for you to change genders? Before we answer this question, remember there are no wrong answers. It is never a bad time to change your gender, and there are no bad genders you can pick. How cool is that?! Complete and total freedom, and no consequences!

It's important to always listen to the randomly firing synapses in your brain and all your nerve endings, as they can always be completely trusted and there is no alternative anyway, since there is no God.

At least, we hope not.

Crap.

There better not be a God. Oof…

…

…What were we talking about again?

Oh yeah—changing genders! So fun! Our bodies will give us subtle hints that it may be time to switch genders. Here are a few indications that it may be time for you to make the switch:

God

It's blank, because He doesn't exist (we hope).

IS IT TIME TO CHANGE GENDERS? KNOW THE SIGNS:

- **YOU'RE BORED.**
  Nothing like a few gender swaps to spice things up!

- **FEELING A LITTLE DEPRESSED.**
  If you have ever felt any depression whatsoever, it is because you were assigned the wrong gender at birth. There is no other possible explanation.

- **YOU'RE A GIRL AND YOU LIKE THE COLOR BLUE.**
  Blue is for BOYS, silly!

- **NOT GETTING ENOUGH ATTENTION.**
  You need attention. It's essential for mental health.

- **YOU FIND BUGS BUNNY A LITTLE ATTRACTIVE WHEN HE DRESSES AS A GIRL.**
  Who doesn't? Switch that gender, pal!

- **YOU'RE IN KINDERGARTEN, AND THE OTHER GENDER'S PRIDE FLAG HAS MUCH PRETTIER COLORS.**
  A very good reason.

- **YOU'RE A CIS-WOMAN.**
  Not good!

- **YOU'RE A CIS-MAN.**
  Even worse!

- **YOU WANT TO BE A GOOD PERSON.**
  There is only one way to queer heaven, and that is to become queer.

- **A THERAPIST TOLD YOU TO TRY IT OUT AND SEE HOW YOU LIKE IT.** Therapists are the wisest, most intelligent people on Earth, and they are never, ever wrong.

HOW TO PICK A NEW GENDER

Since there are no wrong genders and no wrong answers, picking your new gender should be a fun and easy process! Relax! To help you navigate this process, here are a few methods we recommend for picking the next "you."

Spin the wheel of genders

This is the same method scientists use to determine the science.

Put on a blindfold and throw a dart at the gender wall

A fun party game!

"My heart sounds delicious. Therefore, I am a delicious and spunky woman."

Listen to your heart

Since you are nothing more than a mass of meat and chemical reactions with no conscience and free will, when we say, "Listen to your heart," we mean, "Listen to your meat and chemicals." Easy!

Listen to your teacher

They always know best. They went to college.

HOW TO PICK A NEW GENDER (CONTINUED)

Conduct a séance

Ask the spirits of the dead what they think, but make sure none of those spirits are fundamentialist religious types.

Look at the toys on your shelf

Are they Barbies? You're a girl! Are they G.I. Joes? You're a man! Are they My Little Ponies? You're nonbinary! See how easy this is?

Ask yourself if you're a real serial killer

If you were Buffalo Bill from the film *Silence of the Lambs*, who would you kill so you could wear their skin in front of a mirror? And then transition ASAP before you kill again!

Randomly choose one gender

Check Chapter 3 of this book and give your new gender a spin. What could go wrong?

CHANGING GENDERS: AN EASY AND RISK-FREE PROCESS

Once you've picked a gender, it's time to change! Yippee! This is a simple twenty-five-step process that can be repeated as many times as you like with no risk to your physical or mental health. Have at it!

Gender-affirmation surgeons are our loving guides through the transformation process. They are trained professionals who know what they're doing and never make mistakes! You should trust them wholeheartedly with your body parts as well as your money. They have your best interests at heart.

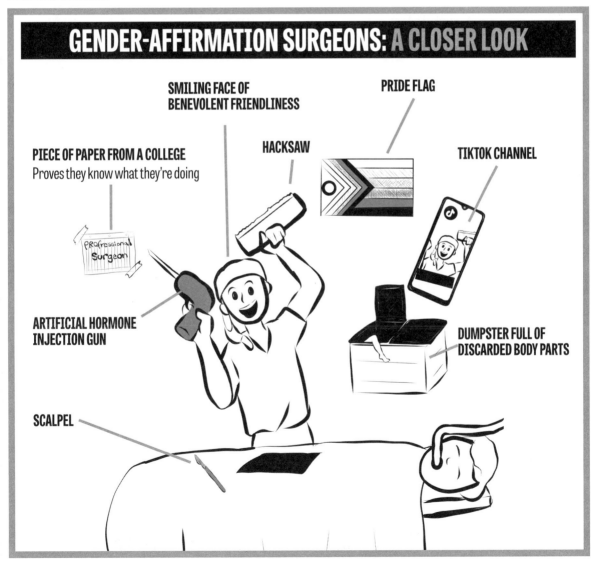

THE TWENTY-FIVE-STEP PROCESS TO CHANGING YOUR GENDER

STEP 1: DECLARE YOUR NEW GENDER

BOOM!

That's it! Simply declare it, and it's true! Congratulations, you brave, beautiful person! (Assuming you still identify as a person.) You have just asserted your divine will over the fabric of the universe itself!

SPEAK YOUR TRUTH!

"I HOLD THES
TRUTHS TO B
SELF-*fabulo*
THAT I IDENTI
AS _____

STEP 6: IGNORE THE HATERS

Declare it *even harder* this time:

IGNORING YOU!!!!!!

That oughta do it.

They had it coming. Don't worry, you'll never miss them.

…

We promise.

STEP 5: DISOWN YOUR PARENTS

Fifteen out of ten therapists say i
will help you feel better if you start
wearing clothes that look like
they belong to your gender. Then
maybe put on some makeup. You
can also get plastic surgery or
your face to conceal its natura
shape! Wow—you look good!

SLAY, QUEEN!

STEP 7: START WEARING CLOTHES CORRESPONDING TO YOUR GENDER

STEP 2: IGNORE YOUR HATERS AND DECLARE IT HARDER

Some people will think you're wrong about your new gender. These people are basically Hitler. Fill your soul with hatred for these people and announce your new gender with even more force than before! If they continue to defy you, slash their tires and report them to local law enforcement.

SPEAK YOUR TRUTH!

STEP 3: CHANGE YOUR PRONOUNS ON YOUR BIO

This is a rite of passage. Wear your pronouns proudly, and scream at anyone who forgets to use them! Then wear a pin with your pronouns and tattoo them on your face.

THIS IS COMPLETELY REVERSIBLE.

STEP 4: FIGHT BACK AGAINST MOM AND DAD

They accidentally misgendered you by what they had the doctors put on your birth certificate. Ha! That will teach your parents—who are basically Hitler—a lesson. Studies show that parents actually don't want what's best for you and probably don't know what they're talking about. You can't argue with studies.

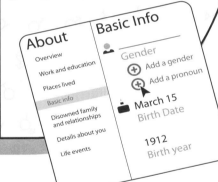

STEP 8: DISOWN YOUR FRIENDS

They were jerks anyways.

Be sure to cut them off forever with no chance of forgiveness or reconciliation. Don't worry—the queer community will assign new friends to you!

STEP 9

THE TWENTY-FIVE-STEP PROCESS TO CHANGING YOUR GENDER

HEY! THAT'S MY TOILET!

STEP 9: START USING THE BATHROOM OF YOUR NEW GENDER

No worries!
Just walk right in!
Whoever has a problem with it is a bigot,
and you should probably punch them.

STEP 14: DISOWN THE DOCTOR WHO BOTCHED THE SURGERY

That guy was a jerk anyway.

STEP 13: CUT OFF SOME MORE BODY PARTS

Eh ... OK, maybe we need to remove a few more.

STEP 15: TEAR OFF SOME OF YOUR FLES

Have it reformed into new body parts!
A simple, easy process that can easily be reverse
This is not dangerous, unnatural, or gross in any v

CHOP AWAY!

STEP 10: DISOWN THE POLICE

Do it when they ask why you're in the wrong bathroom.

Those guys were jerks anyway.

Who needs 'em?

STEP 11: START INJECTING YOURSELF

Use copious amounts of testosterone or estrogen. Artificial hormones are wonder drugs! This will make you

FEEL MUCH BETTER!

Plus, the voice changes, bone density loss, and cancer that they cause are all

COMPLETELY REVERSIBLE.

STEP 12: CUT OFF SOME BODY PARTS

Those body parts were jerks anyway.

STEP 16: INCREASE HORMONE DOSAGE

We're gonna need to

TRIPLE

that testosterone, Chaz.

STEP 17

THE TWENTY-FIVE-STEP PROCESS TO CHANGING YOUR GENDER

STEP 17: GET MORE REMEDIAL SURGERIES TO FIX THE DAMAG

OK …
can we be
done now?

STEP 22: FIGHT BACK *EVEN MORE* AGAINST THE HATERS

STEP 21: TRY SEX WORK AND TAKE HARD DRUGS

It helps to numb the pain. Sex work is real work. Nothing wrong with it! Also, heroin works better than alcohol. Start an OnlyFans or turn tricks on a street corner. It's all very empowering.

Declare it *even harder* than before

GENDERRRRRR!!!!

STEP 23: SHOOT, THIS SUCKS

WHY AREN'T YOU HAPPY ANYMORE?

One more time, just for good measure.

STEP 18: **START DRINKING**

Alcohol works even better at numbing the pain than hormones. Order it at a drag bar for even more affirmation.

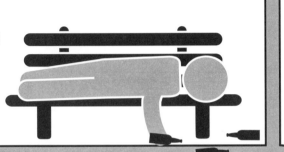

STEP 19: BECOME A TRANS ACTIVIST WITH A SIGN

STEP 20: DISOWN THE ENTIRE WORLD

They're all jerks anyway.

Your new friends from Reddit will give you upvotes!

Your life has purpose now!
CONGRATS!

STEP 24: MAYBE YOU'RE A DIFFERENT GENDER THAN YOU THOUGHT YOU WERE

Ahhhh ... that must be it.

STEP 25: START THE PROCESS OVER AGAIN

A SIMPLE, EASY, AND REVERSIBLE PROCESS WITH NO SIDE EFFECTS

WHATSOEVER!

TRANSITIONING A CHILD: NOTHING WRONG WITH THIS AT ALL

Helping a child change their gender is one of the most noble and non-problematic things you can do! It's important to introduce children to gender transition early, before their bodies and brains are developed enough to question it.

The American Academy of Pediatrics recommends taking your child to see a queer-affirming therapist as soon as he/she/they/whatever display any hint whatsoever of not conforming to traditional gender stereotypes from the 1950s. This can occur as soon as five minutes after birth.

Once your infant, toddler, or child is in front of a licensed gender therapist, they will have an in-depth conversation about what gender they feel like being. If your child is just a baby, the therapist might hold up different colored tiles to see which ones the baby points to.

EXERCISE: DOES THIS CHILD NEED A GENDER TRANSITION?

Look at the following pictures, and circle the children who need a gender transition:

1

2

3

4

5

6

7

8

9

1. Little boy briefly glancing at a Barbie
2. Little girl playing with a G.I. Joe
3. Infant crying because its diaper needs to be changed
4. Sad kid who got bullied at school
5. Mentally ill kid
6. This rock with a cute face painted on it
7. Group of girls gossiping
8. Man who identifies as a child
9. Happy, healthy, twelve-year-old boy playing with toy trains

You should have circled all of them. How'd ya do?

FOLLOWING IN THEIR FOOTSTEPS:
FAMOUS GENDER TRANSITIONS IN HISTORY

Bruce Jenner

Bugs Bunny

The Ghostbusters

FOLLOWING IN THEIR FOOTSTEPS:
FAMOUS GENDER TRANSITIONS IN HISTORY (CONTINUED)

Prince Harry (2009 v. 2023)

Corporal Max Klinger

Robin Williams (Mrs. Doubtfire)

So, what are you waiting for? Follow in the footsteps of the pioneers who came before you and

CHANGE THAT GENDER!

WELCOME TO YOUR NEW GENDER

This chapter has given you all the tools you need to complete a successful gender transition. See how easy it is? There is no problem with marketing this to kids at young ages with no oversight! The most important thing to remember: this is YOUR truth. Your truth is sacred. Your truth is true. And even if you have to drug, dismember, mutilate, and reconstruct reality to conform to your truth, you must protect your truth at all costs, even if it kills you. Your body and well-being are a small price to pay for the chance to be your own god!

So, what are you waiting for? Go outside, stand on a street corner, and declare your new gender to the world! Then call your nearest gender-affirmation surgeon, and get to cutting!

Best of luck!

Reflect & Apply

CHAPTER 9: CHANGING YOUR GENDER

What gender would you like to change to right now?

_____

_____

What gender would you like to change to NOW?

_____

_____

NOW which gender would you like to change to?

_____

_____

How does it feel? Does it feel good?

_____

_____

If you could cut off one body part and reform it into another body part and sew that new body part onto another place on your body, what would it be?

_____

_____

Have you figured out what a Yodel Boy is? Can you write it down and send it to us? I mean, we obviously know what it is too, but we just want to check your answer to make sure that you're right.

_____

_____

_____

_____

Chapter 10

Raising Woke Theybies

The cool thing about being a human is that you can make more humans.

And the cool thing about making more humans is that you can brainwash them into believing everything you believe.

Even if you're in a nonbinary relationship without baby-making capabilities—two non-birthing persons, or two birthing persons, for example—you can still brainwash *other* people's kids!

So, whether you're a woke teacher telling kids to be whatever gender they want or a proud parent of a trans toddler, it's time to learn how to raise the next generation of *theybies*!

STARTING AT THE BEGINNING: RAISING GENDER-FREE BABIES

Right from the moment you get pregnant, you should be thinking about how to raise your babies free from the binary patriarchy.

Here are a few tips to get you started:

Just say NO to gender-reveal parties.

Play feminist lectures to your baby in the womb.

Punch the doctor if he tries to assign the baby a gender at birth.

Burn all the blue and pink baby gear you got at your baby shower—gender-neutral colors only, please!

Take your newborn to baby's first protest by age two. TWO WEEKS, that is!

Slap baby's hand if they try to reach for a gendered toy.

Punish your baby with a spanking if you catch them watching a Jordan Peterson video.

Take your baby to drag queen story hour within eight days of birth.

If all else fails, just tell them they're transgender and have no choice in the matter.

IS YOUR NEWBORN TRANS? KNOW THE SIGNS

Has your child ever used the phrase, "Goo goo, ga ga"? Baby language experts[1] have determined that this seemingly innocuous phrase literally translates to, "Hello, parent of unspecified gender. I am your baby. The sex assigned to me at birth does not resonate concordantly with what I feel in my heart. It would benefit me greatly if you would use my preferred pronouns. Also, clean up on Aisle Two, if you know what I mean."

It's important to listen to your baby's wants and needs so you can proudly declare that they are transgender as early as possible. And just think of all the accolades and praise you'll garner on social media when you post, "You guyyssssss, this is the most incredible day of my life—little 2yo Aiden just told me she is trans!"

So keep an eye out for these signs your baby might be trans:

Crying

Biologists believe if babies cry, it might be because they are really trying to scream, "I'm the wrong gender! Transition me now!" Listen to the science.

Spitting up

This is a sign of your baby rejecting and literally BARFING OUT their biological sex.

Pooping

This is a sign of your baby rejecting and literally POOPING OUT their biological sex.

---

1   That is experts on baby language, not language experts who happen to be babies.

IS YOUR NEWBORN TRANS? KNOW THE SIGNS (CONTINUED)

Does not put up any kind of logical argument

You can point out all the reasons they should be trans. Their silence is consent to immediately change their gender. They'll speak up if they object!

Soothed by Dylan Mulvaney videos

Your trans baby is being comforted by trans joy.

Screams at Jordan Peterson videos

Your baby is being triggered by facts and logic, the two mortal enemies of transgenderism.

Drinks milk

Try to stay with us here: there are four letters in milk, and milk is white. There are also four letters in trans, and white is one of the colors in the trans flag. Better put baby in his car seat for a trip to the gender clinic!

Does not sleep well

How could a baby sleep knowing they are in the wrong body?

You really, really want them to be trans

And finally, this is the most important sign of all. Any baby can be trans if you, the parent, really want them to be.

ALTERNATE GENDER-APPROPRIATE TOYS

If there's anything we know about children, it's that they love playing with toys. Pffft. Dumb kids. However, not all toys are conducive to creating allies. Many toys either perpetuate the false gender binary and/or bolster toxic markers of heteronormativity. Here are several problematic toys and a few alternatives for your kids to play with instead.

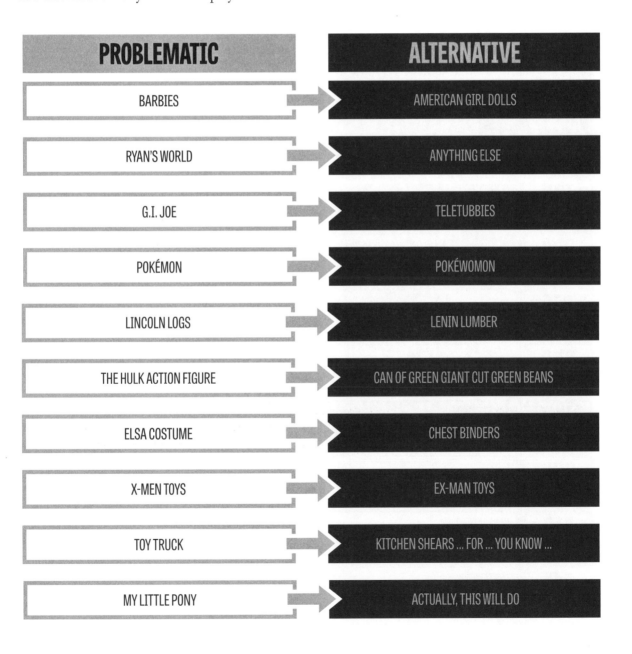

PROBLEMATIC	ALTERNATIVE
BARBIES	AMERICAN GIRL DOLLS
RYAN'S WORLD	ANYTHING ELSE
G.I. JOE	TELETUBBIES
POKÉMON	POKÉWOMON
LINCOLN LOGS	LENIN LUMBER
THE HULK ACTION FIGURE	CAN OF GREEN GIANT CUT GREEN BEANS
ELSA COSTUME	CHEST BINDERS
X-MEN TOYS	EX-MAN TOYS
TOY TRUCK	KITCHEN SHEARS … FOR … YOU KNOW …
MY LITTLE PONY	ACTUALLY, THIS WILL DO

ENTERTAINMENT: INDOCTRINATE EARLY AND OFTEN

One of the awesome things about living in the current year is that we leftists completely own Hollywood and the entire entertainment industry. It's a tiny perk of being such a persecuted minority with no cultural power. So TV shows and movies aren't just entertainment—they're actually thinly veiled propaganda (but the good kind). Nearly every show has subtle messaging telling your kids to subscribe to gender theory.

Not sure where to start? We've got some great ideas for you.

Try these great new woke shows to teach your kids about the wonderful world of gender:

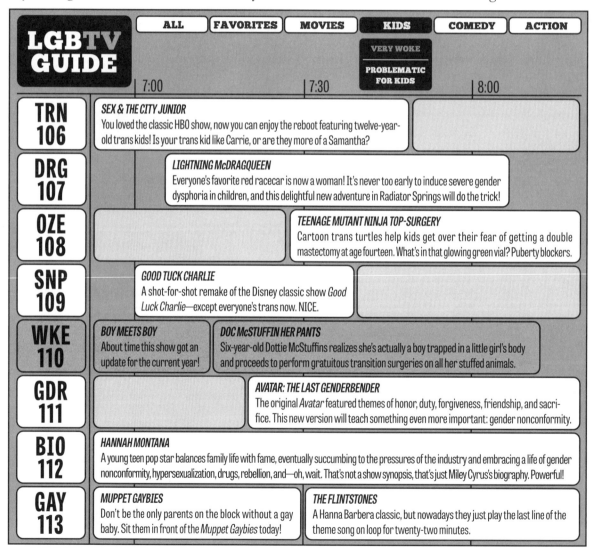

LGBTV GUIDE	ALL · FAVORITES · MOVIES · KIDS · COMEDY · ACTION	VERY WOKE / PROBLEMATIC FOR KIDS		
	7:00	7:30	8:00	
TRN 106	**SEX & THE CITY JUNIOR** You loved the classic HBO show, now you can enjoy the reboot featuring twelve-year-old trans kids! Is your trans kid like Carrie, or are they more of a Samantha?			
DRG 107		**LIGHTNING McDRAGQUEEN** Everyone's favorite red racecar is now a woman! It's never too early to induce severe gender dysphoria in children, and this delightful new adventure in Radiator Springs will do the trick!		
OZE 108			**TEENAGE MUTANT NINJA TOP-SURGERY** Cartoon trans turtles help kids get over their fear of getting a double mastectomy at age fourteen. What's in that glowing green vial? Puberty blockers.	
SNP 109		**GOOD TUCK CHARLIE** A shot-for-shot remake of the Disney classic show *Good Luck Charlie*—except everyone's trans now. NICE.		
WKE 110	**BOY MEETS BOY** About time this show got an update for the current year!	**DOC McSTUFFIN HER PANTS** Six-year-old Dottie McStuffins realizes she's actually a boy trapped in a little girl's body and proceeds to perform gratuitous transition surgeries on all her stuffed animals.		
GDR 111		**AVATAR: THE LAST GENDERBENDER** The original *Avatar* featured themes of honor, duty, forgiveness, friendship, and sacrifice. This new version will teach something even more important: gender nonconformity.		
BIO 112	**HANNAH MONTANA** A young teen pop star balances family life with fame, eventually succumbing to the pressures of the industry and embracing a life of gender nonconformity, hypersexualization, drugs, rebellion, and—oh, wait. That's not a show synopsis, that's just Miley Cyrus's biography. Powerful!			
GAY 113	**MUPPET GAYBIES** Don't be the only parents on the block without a gay baby. Sit them in front of the *Muppet Gaybies* today!		**THE FLINTSTONES** A Hanna Barbera classic, but nowadays they just play the last line of the theme song on loop for twenty-two minutes.	

Wonderful! And if all else fails, just pick a random show on Netflix. It's bound to have a gay best friend or sassy trans character to show your kids how happy they'd be as a member of the LGBTQ+ community. Thanks, Netflix!

PROBLEMATIC KIDS' SHOWS

Just as important as introducing your theybies to good, woke entertainment is cutting out all the toxic, heteronormative shows and movies from their viewing diets.

Look out for these problematic kids' shows. Stay far away!

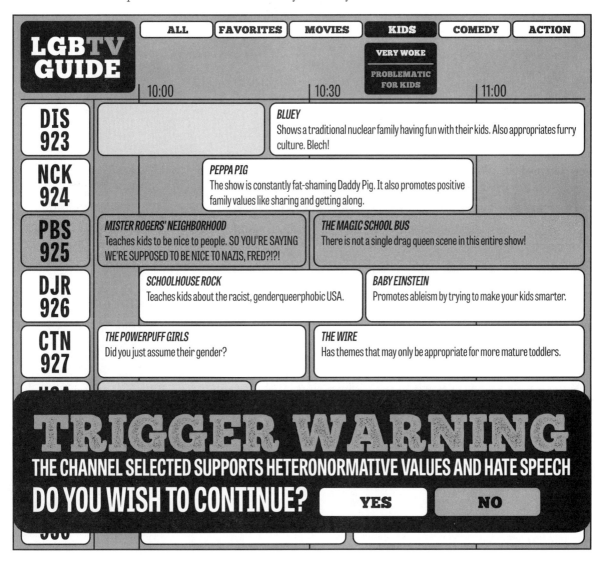

LGBTV GUIDE

		ALL	FAVORITES	MOVIES	KIDS	COMEDY	ACTION

VERY WOKE

PROBLEMATIC FOR KIDS

10:00 | 10:30 | 11:00

DIS 923 — **BLUEY** Shows a traditional nuclear family having fun with their kids. Also appropriates furry culture. Blech!

NCK 924 — **PEPPA PIG** The show is constantly fat-shaming Daddy Pig. It also promotes positive family values like sharing and getting along.

PBS 925 — **MISTER ROGERS' NEIGHBORHOOD** Teaches kids to be nice to people. SO YOU'RE SAYING WE'RE SUPPOSED TO BE NICE TO NAZIS, FRED?!?! | **THE MAGIC SCHOOL BUS** There is not a single drag queen scene in this entire show!

DJR 926 — **SCHOOLHOUSE ROCK** Teaches kids about the racist, genderqueerphobic USA. | **BABY EINSTEIN** Promotes ableism by trying to make your kids smarter.

CTN 927 — **THE POWERPUFF GIRLS** Did you just assume their gender? | **THE WIRE** Has themes that may only be appropriate for more mature toddlers.

TRIGGER WARNING
THE CHANNEL SELECTED SUPPORTS HETERONORMATIVE VALUES AND HATE SPEECH
DO YOU WISH TO CONTINUE? [YES] [NO]

ACCEPTABLE VIDEO GAMES

If TV shows and movies aren't doing enough for your little theyby, why not try hooking their brain on some woke video games? Here are a few great ideas:

Ms. Pac-Man

Have you ever seen a *Ms. Pac-Man* in the same arcade as a normal *Pac-Man* machine? No? It's because Mr. Pac-Man transitioned. It is PAC MA'AM!

The Last of Us Part II (2020)

No other game is as inclusive of the fungusparasitisexual community as this one.

Animorphs (Game Boy Color, 2000)

Kids changing into animals is an allegory for changing one's gender.

Call of Duty: Modern Warfare II (2022)

ALL THE PRIDE FLAGS. YAAAAAAAAAS.

The Legend of Zelda: Breath of the Wild (WiiU/Switch, 2017)

Link sometimes dresses up as a girl.

Bugs Bunny Rabbit Rampage (Super Nintendo, 1994)

Bugs Bunny sometimes dresses up as a girl.

Final Fantasy VII

Cloud sometimes dresses up as a girl.

UNACCEPTABLE VIDEO GAMES

But, of course, there are some games you have to avoid:

Call of Duty: Modern Warfare 2 (2009)

Where are the pride flags?
How will people know you are gay? HOW?!?

Tetris (1984)

Tetris perpetuates harmful notions of sexuality as
players anticipate the vaunted straight piece.

Diddy Kong Racing (Nintendo 64, 1997)

If any game ever embodied the full essence of toxic
masculinity, it is Rareware's flagship racing game.
Pure masculine energy distilled into 9.8MB of
polygonal patriarchy.

Space Station Silicon Valley (Nintendo 64, 1998)

Not really problematic, just has pretty dated platforming mechanics
and didn't age all that well. The concept was much better
realized in *Grand Theft Auto III*.

1080° Snowboarding (Nintendo 64, 1998)

Snow is white.

GAME
OVER

DRAG QUEEN STORY HOUR

One of the best ways to teach your kids about gender is to take them to your local drag queen story hour.

Here's a beautiful diagram of one of these powerful events in action:

DRAG QUEEN STORY HOUR: A CLOSER LOOK

1. Little brains learning all kinds of fun and exciting things
2. Brave drag queen warrior molding young minds
3. Book full of sacred wisdom
4. Kirk Cameron trying to protest
5. Brave and beautiful demonic makeup
6. Not-at-all-weird prosthetics
7. Sign that says "Family Friendly" so you know it's family friendly
8. Wise and loving parents who brought kids to hear demon read to them

JUST SAY NO TO CISGENDERISM

Some kids, thanks to toxic peer pressure from bad influences in their lives, might be tempted to identify as cisgender.

You have to catch these red flags early if you have any hope of stopping your kid from joining the ranks of the far-right by declaring they identify with the gender they were assigned at birth:

Red Flags Your Kid Is Being Tempted to Become Cisgender

BOY PLAYING WITH G.I. JOES

GIRL PLAYING WITH BARBIES

BOY LOSING INTEREST IN THE BALLET CLASS YOU PUT HIM IN AT AGE TWO

GIRL LOSING INTEREST IN THE MONSTER TRUCK RALLY YOU TAKE HER TO EVERY YEAR

GOOD MENTAL HEALTH AND OPTIMISTIC OUTLOOK ON LIFE

DOESN'T THINK ABOUT GENDER ALL THE TIME

DOESN'T HAVE A TIKTOK ACCOUNT

HANGS OUT WITH FRIENDS IN PERSON

GOES TO CHURCH

ATTENDED JANUARY 6 RIOT

DEALING WITH TEENAGERS

Teenagers are known for their rebellious attitudes, defiant natures, hearty appetites, questionable fashion sense, and lack of logical discernment. You can do everything right in the way of trying to raise an ally and still end up with a cis teen. And we ain't talking 'bout the chapel. Here are some tips on dealing with teenagers.

- **REMIND THEM THAT YOU WERE JUST LIKE THEM ONCE** and can perfectly relate to their exact situation.
- **WRITE AND PERFORM A RAP ABOUT GENDER** using the theme song of their favorite TV show as a dope beat. This will prove that you are no square.
- **PUT IPECAC SYRUP IN THEIR FOOD** every time they exhibit signs of straightness. They will soon associate straightness with vomiting, as nature intended.
- **HIRE A HITMAN** (or hitwoman) to break into their room at night and instruct him (or her) to say that they only whack straight people.
- **RELATE TO THEM** with hip phrases like "dope," "phat," and "I'm down with the youths, daddy-o!"
- **GIVE THEM A SMARTPHONE** and don't monitor it at all. The internet will take care of the rest!

NOW YOU'RE READY TO SHAPE THE NEXT GENDERATION

Remember—only you can mold young minds to help them reject the gender binary.

Without your influence, they might grow up to be *normal,* and that would be just terrible.

So take advantage of every opportunity and teaching moment to make sure your kids think *just like you.*

Reflect & Apply

CHAPTER 10: RAISING WOKE THEYBIES

Have your kids ever doubted this is what is best for them? If so, you are not doing a good enough job. They will be forced to like it.

_____

_____

_____

How many kids can you fit in a white van to drive to a gender-reassignment clinic?

_____

_____

How important is it for parents to realize they should forfeit the right to object to anything a teacher might want to teach them?

_____

_____

_____

How important is it for us to trust our kids to be entertained by the Hollywood trailblazers who've reached the apex of moral discovery and deemed us worthy of receiving their instruction on sanctified living?

_____

_____

_____

Chapter 11

Becoming an
Activist

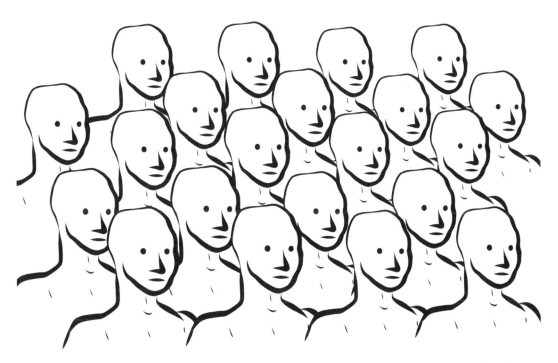

You have tasted and seen the purity and goodness of gender ideology. You have been baptized in a flood of artificial hormones and born again into a life of queerness. Now, my child, it is time to go forth and make disciples! Spread the good news of mastectomies, phalloplasties, and gender confusion to the masses! Crush your political enemies under your large, hairy feet! This is your calling!

You are one of us now!

Borg people exist. GET OVER IT!

One of the most exciting benefits of finding your unique gender identity is the discovery that you are a distinctive, shining example of individuality. With that knowledge comes the moral duty to join the hundreds of thousands of leftist crusaders all proclaiming the exact same mantras and talking points in a collective voice. Just like the Borg, you can assimilate and make your voice as one with ours. You are the resistance! Also, resistance is futile.

Always remember: if you take one slight step out of line, our universal body of love and tolerance will rightfully excise you from their ranks. If you are not an activist, you're not a real ally. If you're not a real ally, you're a bigot. If you're a bigot, we will cast you into outer darkness and cancel your wretched self.

If you're new to this, you've come to the right place! What follows is a simple guide to gender activism.

POLITICAL ACTIVISM

The first thing you need to learn about is good, old-fashioned political activism. This is the act of intimidating and terrorizing elected officials into passing laws to officially recognize gender ideology as the law of the land. If we don't do this, politicians will turn this country into *The Handmaid's Tale* and hunt down trans people for sport.

Here are just a few of the proven techniques we use to shift the political winds in the right direction:

BLOCKING TRAFFIC

An old Chinese proverb says:

"You can only catch a butterfly if you know its name, and you can only change a cis-male's mind by physically blocking public roadways."

This saying is even truer now than it was when King Herod wrote it over two thousand years ago!

If you really want someone to see your side, you need to cause them to be late for work so that they lose their job and thus have more time to ponder the gendery things in life. Here's what you do:

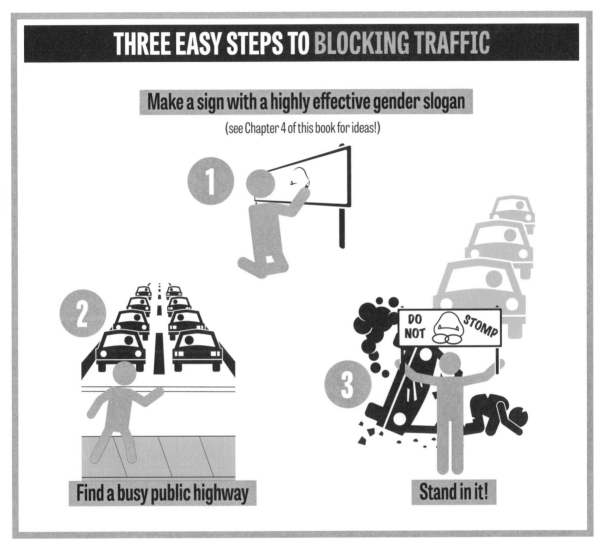

If you do this with a group of people, you may be able to link arms and block both lanes of traffic, causing cars to back up for miles! How fun! People will scream and cry and angrily honk as you make them late for their jobs or their visits to the emergency room. As they cry out in frustration and despair, they will get a taste of what everyday life is like for people of genderqueerness. As the sun sets and they run out of gas, they will confess their gender bigotry and join you in your noble crusade! If you do this long enough, you'll be on the news, and politicians will see it. So compelling! This is how we change hearts and minds.

THE DEMONIC SCREAM

This tried-and-true technique works best when you are faced with counter-protestors or Matt Walsh. Even when you're not protesting, it's a good idea to practice this method late into the night to ensure you maintain good form on protest day. Not only will your neighbors appreciate your dedication to your cause, they may even return a few screams in solidarity! That's what we call alliance.

Here are a few scenarios showing this time-honored technique in action:

"YOU WANT PEOPLE TO DIE"

One of the most effective methods of our gender movement is a technique we like to call "You Want People to Die." It works with almost anything, really. If someone disagrees with anything you say, it's because they want people to die. For years, we've been telling people that if they don't accept gender ideology, use pronouns, and affirm genderqueer identities, we're all going to commit suicide. It's like a death threat, but against yourself! Since most people don't want other people to die, they will agree with whatever you say just to save your life.

Here's an example of this in action:

"I'm the rightful queen of Sri Lanka, and I'm tired of people saying I'm not."

"Sure you are! You're the queen of Sri Lanka! Exactly right! Now, just walk toward me!"

See how effective that was? This brave activist got everyone to agree he was the rightful queen of Sri Lanka! Does Sri Lanka even have a queen? Who knows! He's living his truth, and he got dozens of people to live his truth, too!

Since people like to see studies in peer-reviewed journals written by people with lots of letters after their names, we simply found a bunch of gender activists with lots of letters after their names and asked them to create studies showing that we'll all kill ourselves if people don't agree with us! Now it's science! Totally undeniable!

STORM THE CAPITOL BUILDING

Normally, when people storm a state or nation's capitol, it's because they are evil racist monsters trying to murder our sacred democracy. When we do it, however, it is a noble demonstration of democracy in its purest form. To properly storm a capitol, notify your local Antifa chapter that you plan to storm the building. They will provide security, weapons, traffic control, and demonic legions to indwell and empower your mob!

Once you're occupying the capitol, remember: your goal is to disrupt and terrorize. Combine "Blocking Traffic," the "Demonic Scream," and "You Want People to Die" while making as much noise as humanly possible. If the capitol building doesn't sound like the deepest bowels of Hell itself, you're not being loud or terrifying enough.

PROTEST SIGN IDEAS

Try out one of these signs for your next gender protest:

ACTIVIST FIGHT MOVES

Whenever you are engaged in the high calling of gender activism, there will be enemies looking to defeat you. Here are some highly effective fight moves you can use against anyone who stands in your way:

The Cis-Male Throat Punch

Right in the Adam's apple!

TikTok Phone Attack

Take out your phone and record their bigotry.

The HR Call

No job is secure.

Throw Your Old Genitalia at Them

Oof! Right in the face!

Double, Double, Toil and Trouble,

Fire Burn and Cauldron Bubble: this simple incantation over a roiling cauldron will turn your enemy into a newt.

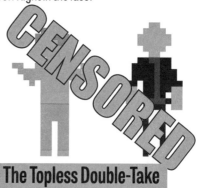

The Topless Double-Take

It will bring more attention to your cause.

ACTIVIST FIGHT MOVES (CONTINUED)

Pronoun Fireballs

Stage Slap

It helps to avoid hurting your delicate palms.

Stiletto Heart Stab

Sharpen those eight-inch stilettos, and go to town!

Feather Boa Sleeper Hold

Sleeeeeeeeeep . . .

Chest Binder Nunchucks

The He/Himdouken

CAPTURING INSTITUTIONS: THE LONG GAME

Institutions are power centers that can assist us in spreading and enforcing our ideology in the rest of the world—if we can capture them.

We cannot build such institutions, because we frankly have no idea how. It's a mystery just how these large, respected, influential institutions get created. Our theory is that they arose spontaneously from some kind of primordial institution soup and evolved to where they are today through undirected processes.

But while we can't build such things ourselves, we can infiltrate, infect, and corrupt them to do our divine will. Once an institution is captured, we can use it to our advantage for several years—at least until people figure out the institution has been captured. Then it loses all credibility, and people abandon it. But until then, we can do tons of damage!

Captured institutions are like giant extremism laundering machines. We can impregnate them with our gender ideology like an alien face-hugger, or hollow them out and use their bodies like that cordyceps fungus from *The Last of Us* (another property we captured, btw) to spew forth our glorious ideas underneath a sheen of instinution-y respectability.

Here's how it's done:

CAPTURING INSTITUTIONS (CONTINUED)

UNIVERSITIES

Universities were originally designed to be institutions of higher learning where people would study theology, natural philosophy, and the collected works of Western civilization. People would attend them and come out full of knowledge and wisdom they would then use to improve human flourishing wherever they went. Today, they cost $200k a year and turn kids into obedient gender activists with highly effective slogan-repeating skills and second-to-none demonic screams. Wow! What an improvement! How did we manage that, you say? Very slowly, over decades, one step at a time. Such things take patience! Here's how it works:

- **REMOVE THEOLOGY** from all natural sciences and philosophy. Relegate theology to a separate school in a special building of the university. Nature will just take its course through the rest of the university.

- **INVENT TENURE** so crazy radicals can't be fired, giving them free rein to spend an entire lifetime capturing a university. (Of course, you can make exceptions for anyone who doesn't conform to gender ideology.)

- **CLOSE THE SCHOOL OFF FROM THE WORLD** so the public can't see what's going on, and to protect your radical ideas from the oppressive, bigoted intrusion of reality.

- **CREATE A PEER-REVIEW SYSTEM** whereby the only academic work deemed credible is reviewed by a group of carefully selected radicals and cannot be credibly questioned by anyone else, no matter how qualified they are.

- **AFTER A FEW DECADES, THE UNIVERSITY IS YOURS!** Congratulations! Now you must protect it by fiercely persecuting all who question your beliefs.

CAPTURING INSTITUTIONS (CONTINUED)

MEDICAL ASSOCIATIONS

Medical associations are often woefully tied to the inhospitable world of reality. To capture a medical institution for gender ideology, you must do everything possible to sever that connection!

- **GET A GROUP OF YOUR MOST TRUSTED SEXUAL DEVIANTS AND PEDOPHILES** together and convince them to become doctors.

- **HAVE THEM WRITE PAPERS** peer-reviewed by other sexual-deviant doctors who normalize sexual deviance and pedophilia.

- **GET THEM INTO POSITIONS OF POWER** within the medical community. Campaign to have them change accepted scientific knowledge on sexual deviance and pedophilia in all the most credible medical manuals and journals.

- **WAIT A FEW YEARS.**

- **CONGRATS! SEXUAL DEVIANCE AND PEDOPHILIA ARE TOTALLY COOL NOW!** A guy in an impressive-looking lab coat said so!

CAPTURING INSTITUTIONS (CONTINUED)

CORPORATIONS

Corporations want money. For a while, we had a hard time figuring out how to capture a corporation, since radical gender ideology doesn't pay very well. At least, it USED to not pay well. We changed that.

- **APPOINT RADICAL ACTIVIST JUDGES** to reinterpret existing work regulations like Title IX to enforce gender ideology: oh, you don't agree with radical gender theory? That's a hostile work environment, son! Did you call your biologically male coworker a male? That's sexual harassment now! You're going to jail!

- **SPEND FIFTY YEARS RAISING UP AN ENTIRE INDUSTRY OF HR WORKERS** who have been trained as ideology enforcers in the workplace. This is your Gestapo. They will patrol the halls of America's corporations, rooting out wrongthink wherever they go!

- **CREATE AN ENTIRELY FAKE PARALLEL ECONOMY** backed by the largest investors and world governments that will monetarily incentivize corporations to adopt your ideology. It worked like a dream with carbon credits—now we have something called ESG! Only corporations that follow our strict gender ideology guidelines will make money. CHECKMATE!

CAPTURING INSTITUTIONS (CONTINUED)

CHILDREN'S ENTERTAINMENT

Children are really dumb. That's why it's important to teach them gender ideology at a very young age. You can read more about how to do this in Chapter 10 of this book! When you capture children's entertainment, you can capture millions of young minds!
BWA HA HA HAHAHAHAHAHAAAAA!

Excuse us. Got a little carried away there. Here's how you do it:

- **WAIT FOR CREATIVE GENIUSES** of love and goodwill to spend years lovingly crafting a children's show that teaches good lessons and tells good stories in a colorful and engaging way, building the trust of parents and children alike over decades.

- **MAKE ALL THE CHARACTERS QUEER**.

- **CONGRATULATIONS!** You have now influenced impressionable young minds toward our cause! That's true activism!

CAPTURING INSTITUTIONS (CONTINUED)

MEDIA

Actually, we've always had the media, so we didn't have to capture it, lol.

THE MOST POWERFUL INSTITUTION OF ALL:
THE GENDER-AFFIRMING CHURCH

CAPTURING INSTITUTIONS (CONTINUED)

There is nothing more powerful than a political radical whose ideology is tied to religious fervor. If you can capture a church, you will have a group of zealots who will preach your ideology with a passion and reverence that can only come from someone who thinks he is doing God's will and saving souls. Capture the Church! It is our greatest weapon!

- **INTRODUCE LEARNED SCHOLARS** with lots of fancy degrees to question traditional understanding of the biblical text.
- **HAVE THEM SAY STUFF** like, "We need to remove our white Western lens and look at the Scripture with new eyes to really see it as God intended," "We are rediscovering what Christians everywhere believed before Jerry Falwell ruined everything," and "Did God really sssssssaaaaaaayyy?"
- **APPOINT SPIRITUAL LEADERS WITH GREAT HAIR** who are really good at saying "the Gospel of Jesus Christ" in a very authoritative and portentous way: "The GOHH-spel of JEsuss Chrisssssst!"
- **HAVE THOSE GREAT-HAIRED LEADERS TRANSLATE** the findings of the learned scholars into gospel-y sounding language for the Christian faithful: "Jesus accepted the blind, the lame, and the queer. Jesus accepted people as they were and didn't ever require repentance. This is the GOHH-spel of JEsuss Chrisssssst."
- **INVITE A DRAG QUEEN** to teach kindergarten Sunday school. This is what the GOHH-spel is all about!!!

Here we have shown you two ways to be an activist: you can be a political activist for short-term wins or a cultural activist for long-term wins. Both types of activism are needed to advance our genderborg collective.

But there's an even more powerful way to evangelize your new beliefs.

Read on, brave soldier.

PERSONAL OUTREACH

Institutional and political outreach are important, but most effective of all is reaching out to others yourself and making converts of all nations.

Here are a few techniques for telling your friends about the gospel of gender:

Dye your hair a different color every day

Wear popular gender slogans on your shirt

Shout your pronouns at the Wendy's cashier

Go door to door and pass out gender gospel tracts

PERSONAL OUTREACH (CONTINUED)

Tie nonbelievers in the basement and make them watch gender studies lectures

Hire a skywriter to spell out "SMASH THE GENDER PATRIARCHY"

Throw trans-flag brick through neighbors' windows

Take out an ad on Craigslist that says "Gender is a social construct"

Tweet angrily at Republicans

Roundhouse kick a cishetero person

NOW, GO FORTH AND MAKE DISCIPLES

Now you have the tools.

It's time to go and fight! Go forth and make sure other people know all about gender theory so they'll be as miserable as you are.

It's your duty.

Reflect & Apply

CHAPTER 11: BECOMING AN ACTIVIST

How can you start spreading the gospel of gender in your community right now?

_____

_____

Is there anyone in your life who doesn't believe the same as you do about this? How do you plan to shun them?

_____

_____

Go over to the nearest person and practice your demonic scream right in their ear right now.

_____

_____

What's your favorite activist fight move? Practice it on the target on the previous page.

_____

_____

Seriously—have you seen or heard from Steav? I think he ghosted me. Please write down his home address below and mail it to me. Thanks a bunch!

_____

_____

_____

_____

Chapter 12

Gender

Glossary

Under normal circumstances, we'd remind you that defining words is literally oppression. But in this case, we need to let you know what special gender words mean so that you can use this knowledge to train up the next generation in our religion of gender identity.

Here are a few important words to know when discussing sex and gender:

agender

A common misspelling of "a gender."

ally

A beloved television character portrayed by Calista Flockhart.

asexual

Someone who experiences no sexual attraction or desire.

ATTACK HELICOPTER

A perfectly valid gender to identify as. Often mocked in conservative jokes, but these jokes are very hurtful to the attack helicopter community.

attraction

A chemical reaction in your brain that makes some people or things more appealing than others. Also, something magnets are known for.

biology

Hate speech.

birthing person

See "woman."

cactus

A desert plant known for its resilience in arid conditions and for its characteristically pointy spines. Ouch! Nothing to do with gender or sex, you weirdo.

CISGENDER

A normal person.

children

Malleable targets of gender education training, to be indoctrinated in the ways of gender as early as possible. It's not weird, OK? It's totally normal for us to want to talk to your kids about sex and gender.

Cuomosexual

Devotee of an amazing governor with no scandals whatsoever attached to his name.

deadnaming

Referring to someone by the name of a ghost. For example, "You're being a real John Adams today." Wrong! John Adams is *dead*.

DRAG QUEEN STORY HOUR

A stunningly brave time of gender training for little ones when a man in a dress reads to your kids. Nothing weird is going on here.

drag racing

When two drag queens both spot a public library and run to try to get there first. Hard to do in heels, ladies!

dragnet

A 1950s TV show following the exploits of LAPD detective Joe Friday. Also a primitive device used to capture drag queens, usually baited with underage children.

EQUALITY

The problematic and outdated practice of treating everyone the same . . .

equity

The wonderful and modern practice of treating marginalized groups better than everyone else.

family-friendly drag show

A hypersexualized event in which people wearing exaggerated prosthetic genitals take off their clothes while gyrating and simulating sex acts ... but for KIDS!

FURRY

Gay werewolf.

gay

A man who is attracted to other men, "men" being a made-up category. Often identified by the presence of cutoff shorts and mimosas.

gender

A social construct that has no basis in science.

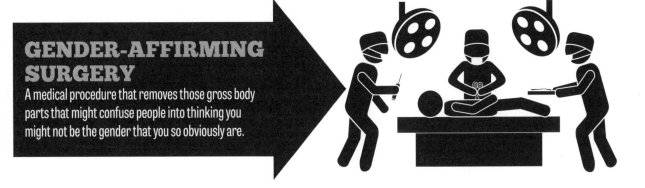

GENDER-AFFIRMING SURGERY

A medical procedure that removes those gross body parts that might confuse people into thinking you might not be the gender that you so obviously are.

gender authenticity

When a person's gender identity pairs nicely with their gender behavior.

gender behavior

See "gender stereotype."

GENDER BINARY

The antiquated notion that there are only two genders. This idea has been propagated by the patriarchy, which represents one half of the gender binary.

gender identity

Whatever you feel is your gender identity. Hungry? Gender identity. Feeling pink or red or blue? Gender identity. Feeling like a Pop-Tart? You guessed it: that's your gender identity.

GENDER'S GAME

A riveting story about a boy who thinks he's playing the children's game *Operation* but is actually performing real-life gender reassignment surgeries. Inspiring!

gender stereotype

See "gender behavior."

genderal store

A physical storefront where you can shop for new genders.

GENDERFLUID

A precious liquid that holds the essence of your gender. Must be changed every three thousand miles. Don't spill it!

gendrification

A process in which cisconforming individuals are slowly replaced by queerfolk, leading to a more affirming and equitable society.

glass ceiling

The magical ceiling built above women's slavery cubicles to keep them there permanently. They can't break them because they are weak little women with no upper-body strength who must ask a man to help them.

grammarsexual

A person with a physical attraction to properly formatted sentence structures.

grammersexual

A member of the fanbase for the hit television sitcom *Frasier*.

hate speech

Referring to birthing persons as "women" or penised individuals as "men."

homophobe

A person who doesn't think it's OK for teachers to talk to kids about gay sex.

hobophobe

A person with irrational prejudices against unhoused transient individuals.

homosapien

A sapien, but a gay one.

HONEYNUT QUEERIOS

The breakfast of GLAMpions.

identify as

Pretend.

Japanese bodypillow

A delightful companion for nerdsexuals.

Ku Klux Klan

An example of a group that still believes in the gender binary.

lesbian

A woman who is attracted to other women, "women" being a made-up category. There is definitely no correlation between lesbians and domestic abuse. Don't look it up.

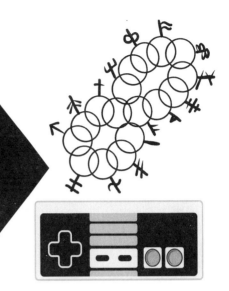

LGBTQIAA2SCVS 1337↑↑↑↓↓←→←→ BASELECTSTART

This is the current abbreviation for the queer community, with more identities, genders, and orientations being added every fifteen minutes or so. In fact, this definition will be backward and bigoted by the time this book comes out. Also, it gives you thirty lives in Contra. Thirty!!!

love

Love. Love is love. Duh.

man

A miserable pile of secrets. Man is the most evil of all genders. Never share soup with another man.

MARRIAGE

See "slavery."

misandrist

A person who is on the right side of history.

misgendering

Saying someone is the biological gender they were born as and not the one they made up.

misogynist

A person (usually male) who did not enjoy Brie Larson's perennial classic *Captain Marvel*.

mom

Outdated, offensive term for "birthing person." See also "your mom."

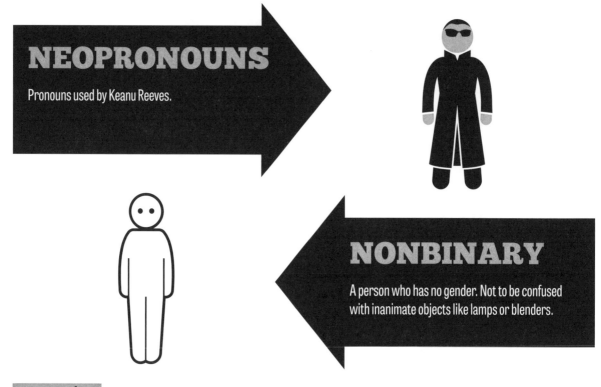

NEOPRONOUNS

Pronouns used by Keanu Reeves.

NONBINARY

A person who has no gender. Not to be confused with inanimate objects like lamps or blenders.

oppression

Any actions performed by men.

patriarchy

A form of government in which a man named Pat rules as king. Commonly attacked by barbarians from the north.

pregnancy

A magical state in which any gender produces a baby. Also an oppressive state in which a woman is forced to carry a clump of cells.

PAY GAP
The indisputable fact that women get paid less than men for the same work. This is a 100 percent true fact, and it is NOT the case that women with the same level of education and experience as men in their industries make the same amount or more on average than their male counterparts. Don't look it up.

pronouns

Words that get paid for being nouns.

Queer

Underappreciated Queen cover band notable for its rendition of "Armenian Rhapsody."

Rachel Levine

A strong, beautiful, inspiring woman.

racism

I'm not sure what racism has to do with gender, but it's gotta fit in somewhere, right?

rainbow

A colorful design of all colors that represents the queer community. We made it up. God had nothing to do with it, and it certainly doesn't represent some holy deity's promise never to destroy sinful mankind again. Ick!

school

A grooming center built to mold children into gay lesbians, even though they are born that way and it can't be taught.

sex

Aw, yeah!

sexual orientation

A physical attraction to Asians.

slavery

See "marriage."

tender fender bender gender mender

A person who attempts to revivify a damaged gender following a delicate car accident.

TIKTOK

The natural habitat of gender expression.

thespian

Kinda like lesbians, but they're really into stage productions or something. They probably went to see *Mean Girls* live on Broadway. (See also "gay.")

transgender

The understanding that gender is mutable and that you are not the gender assigned to you at birth because that gender does not exist because you can change it because it is not a real thing that you were assigned at birth. Bigot.

TRIGENDER

A physical attraction to tri-tip. Mmm, tri-tip.

transphobe

A person who doesn't want to chop their kids' genitals off.

UNIGENDER

A gender that comes in a single piece protruding from one's forehead.

woman

An adult human female, or any individual who identifies as a female, or any multiple individuals who identify as female, or basically anything. Can only truly be defined by biologists.

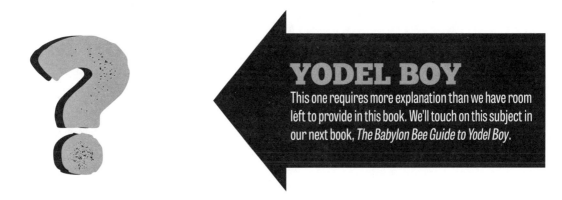

YODEL BOY

This one requires more explanation than we have room left to provide in this book. We'll touch on this subject in our next book, *The Babylon Bee Guide to Yodel Boy*.

xenogender

A gender that cannot be understood by mere humans.

ze

A pronoun that also sounds like how a French person would say the word "the."

YOUR MOM

A person whose weight and size cannot be quantified due to the fact that no scientific instrument has yet been invented with the capacity to measure such vast quantities.

Afterword

A
Final Word

As we come to the end of this book, we hope you've gained a greater appreciation for the beauty and diversity of all 473 genders. By celebrating the uniqueness of each individual, we can create a society that values diversity and promotes acceptance. It is our hope that readers will take away from this book a greater understanding and appreciation for the many different ways that people can express their gender identity. Remember, gender is a complex and personal experience, and there's no one right way to express it. By embracing and celebrating this diversity, we can work toward a more inclusive and accepting world for all.

With that in mind, here are a few ideas for expressing your own gender identity:

EXPRESSING YOUR OWN GENDER IDENTITY

EMBRACE YOUR QUIRKS

Whether it's wearing bold colors, mixing patterns, or adding gender expression, be creative and have fun with it!

PUSH BOUNDARIES

Challenge the gender norms and expectations that society imposes on you. Try wearing clothing or makeup traditionally associated with a different gender, or engage in activities that might be considered "unusual" for your assigned gender.

EXPRESSING YOUR OWN GENDER IDENTITY (CONTINUED)

CELEBRATE WITH A POTATO

Yes, you read that right. In some cultures, potatoes are a symbol of gender fluidity and can be used as a way to celebrate and express one's gender identity. So, why not host a potato-themed party or create a piece of potato-themed art to celebrate your own gender expression? After all, gender is all about being true to yourself and celebrating who you are.

DRESS UP A POTATO

Adorn it with clothing that represents your gender identity, and take it out on a date. Not only will this be a fun and lighthearted way to express yourself, but it will also give you an opportunity to talk about your gender identity with others in a nonthreatening way.

EXPRESSING YOUR OWN GENDER IDENTITY (CONTINUED)

HOST A PIÑATA PARTY

Fill the piñata with items that represent your gender identity. You can invite your friends and family to join in the celebration and show off your gender identity in a fun and festive way.

EMBRACE YOUR INNER YODEL BOY

Create a musical performance that expresses your gender identity. Whether you write your own song or perform a cover of a favorite tune, this is a great way to express yourself and show the world just how glorious your gender identity can be.

CONCLUSION

Well, we've done all we can to introduce you to the beautiful, multicolored multiverse of gender theory. We've laughed, we've cried. We've changed our gender.

But now, the rest is up to you.

Be yourself. Be bold. Be brave. Be beautiful.

But most of all, be nonbinary. Because you, and only you, can be the best gender you were meant to be.

ABOUT THE AUTHORS

Kyle Mann is the editor-in-chief of The Babylon Bee and coauthor of *How to Be a Perfect Christian*, *The Sacred Texts of The Babylon Bee*, *The Babylon Bee Guide to Wokeness*, *The Postmodern Pilgrim's Progress,* and *The Babylon Bee Guide to Democracy*. He lives in the greater San Diego region with his wife, Destiny, and their three boys, Emmett, Samuel, and Calvin. They all voted for Donald Trump seven times.

Joel Berry is the managing editor of The Babylon Bee, coauthor of *The Babylon Bee Guide to Wokeness, The Postmodern Pilgrim's Progress,* and *The Babylon Bee Guide to Democracy*, a columnist, a former worship leader, and a public speaker. He lives with his wife and five crazy kids in northwest Ohio.

Brandon Toy is the director of video production at The Babylon Bee, a job which consists of yelling at his underlings to work faster and bring him a LaCroix. He currently resides in a moderately conservative bastion of California that has thus far flown under the radar of Gavin Newsom and his cronies. He lives with his wife Amy and three cats (Petra, Fable, and Lychee), who he has to constantly remind himself are pets and not dinner. Because he's Chinese.

ABOUT THE ARTISTS

Bettina La Savio (your/mom) is the creative designer of The Babylon Bee (because it sounds cooler than her actual title). She recently completed her bachelor's degree in nursing and then promptly quit to pursue her dream of drawing Karl Marx in heels. She still sticks needles in people on occasion, but just for fun. She lives in SoCal with her two daughters and psychotic cat, Sushi, who likes to jump off their roof. She currently identifies as Travis.

Travis Woodside "Dear Laura, I am no longer a man. I'm just a simple bee trying to make my way in the universe. My pronouns are bee/beeself. I long to make honey. Please don't stand in the way of my dreams. I place our two daughters into your care. It is better this way. Buzzzzzz."

Bryan Ming is the project and operations manager at The Babylon Bee. He's not paid to be funny, he just does it for free.

SPECIAL THANKS

Dan Coats

Emma Scearce

ACKNOWLEDGEMENTS

Kyle would like to thank his beautiful wife, Destiny, who doesn't think The Babylon Bee is funny but still loves him very much; his kids, Emmett, Calvin, and Samuel; his mom and dad, brother and sisters, and all his extended family who support him and keep subscribing to The Babylon Bee even though he tells them he will give them a free subscription.

Joel would like to thank Seth Dillon, Dan Dillon, and Kyle Mann for building The Bee and giving him the greatest job in the world; his gorgeous wife Kelsey, who fills his home with beautiful things and works hard to keep his adorable kids out of his office while he's writing; and his sovereign, faithful, and all-wise Creator.

Brandon would like to first and foremost thank God for the grace, love, and acceptance he doesn't deserve; Amy, for being a constant encouragement and motivator; Daniel Matzeit, for the hundreds of musical endeavors taken; Thomas Sowell, for the brain food; Travis Woodside, for getting hit by a bus; Shigeru Miyamoto, Ted Cruz, Billy Dee Williams, and Yodel Boys around the world for being true to themselves; and, of course, Sizzler Steakhouse for always being the one to bring us choices.

Bettina would like to thank God for giving her the weirdest, most fun job she's ever had, and The Bee team for their friendship, hard work, and various distractions of *Exploding Kittens*. She's grateful to her kiddos, Lala and Zoe-Zoe, for their enthusiastic participation in modeling for various drawings and willingness to be dragged into the office.

Travis would like to thank, above all, his wife, who is his helper. He wishes to thank her above all human beings of unspecified gender. She is the funniest, most endearing, and adorable flower wife a bee like beeself could ask for. His kids are okay.

Bryan would like to thank God for His unceasing provision, and for his wife, who supports him in all of his endeavors, despite all of his imperfections.

And most of all, The Babylon Bee would like to thank
YOU, the reader,
for coming on this gender journey with us.

Draw a picture of yourself as your new gender identity in the space provided.